UNITED MEN OF HONOR PRESENTS:

UNITED MEN OF HONOR
OVERCOMING ADVERSITY THROUGH FAITH

VISIONARY AUTHOR

KEN A. HOBBS II

World Publishing and Productions

United Men of Honor: Overcoming Adversity Through Faith

©Copyright 2022 United Men of Honor

ISBN: 978-1-957111-06-3

DEDICATION

This book is dedicated to the Man of Honor in my life—my father, my hero, and my friend. I will always love you, Dad!! I miss you every day.

–Ken

CONTENTS

INTRODUCTION

You are about to dive into one of the most encouraging books you will ever read. It is filled with stories of men who have overcome adversity through faith and claimed victory in some of life's most difficult battles. These men have become men of honor, warriors, leaders, and heroes, willing to share their message of hope and faith.

As the enemy does his best to take men out and off their mission, the war he instigates rages on in men's lives around the world. Where have the "mighty men" gone? This world needs more men to step up, step out, and be men of honor. They need to be warriors for their faith, their family, their community, and their country. And they need to be strong for the weak, leading them with courage to be overcomers. This book has been written to proclaim the stories of God's overwhelming provision and care and share His Word with you and with the world.

We are each a work in progress, trying to accomplish great and mighty things in our lifetime. Some of us may currently have issues and challenges we need to overcome before we can see a breakthrough. Some may need to see a manifestation of God's power over circumstances or consequences of decisions in our lives. Others may be ready to proudly step forward and profoundly claim victory, sharing what God is doing in their own life.

Wherever you may be on your journey, we pray this book will encourage and empower you to overcome your adversities with faith and take hold of the victory God has planned just for you. We believe each man alive on this planet can be a victorious overcomer in whatever situation life brings his way. Yes, God is awakening warriors to step up and be heard as they live with boldness and courage as overcomers.

We need not worry or be stressed in any trials or tragedies of life because our sword (God's Word) is clear about overcoming any situation.

> Yet even in the midst of all these things, we triumph over them all, for God has made us to be more than conquerors, and his demonstrated love is our glorious victory over EVERYTHING! (Romans 8:37 TPT, emphasis added)

As you read, get ready to be empowered to be an Overcomer of Adversity and accomplish it through Faith as you become a man who honors and a Man of Honor!

"Armor Up, be FIT to Fight, you've got what it takes...."

KEN A. HOBBS II

 Ken A. Hobbs II is a Christ follower, devoting his life to impacting others in para-church ministries, missions, and his business, where he leads a marketplace ministry.

Ken is the Founder of United Men of Honor— leading, coaching, and motivating men to become men of God in their homes, businesses, and communities.

Ken is also part of the Leadership Team of Band of Brothers. He is strongly passionate about the bootcamps and believes they are needed in this world so that men do not have to fight their struggles alone. www.BandofBrothersFL.com

Ken Hobbs II is a Senior Vice President/ Financial Coach Multiple Brokerage owner and operator for www.PRImerica.com/kenhobbs2 — impacting communities nationwide with business-building, coaching/training, and personal financial coaching and services.

Ken is married to his wife Kimberly and actively supports her in the women's ministry, Women World Leaders. www.WomenWorldLeaders.com

Ken's work also reaches around the world, where he supports Kerus Global Education, African Orphan Care Project as an Advisory Board member. He is also the event coordinator for Encounter Nights of Palm Beach. For more information, visit www.healingencounternights.com

Ken is a father, grandfather, and uncle who passionately loves his family and friends.

UNITED MEN OF HONOR TOGETHER WE CAN.

THE INFLUENCE OF A MAN OF HONOR

BY KEN A. HOBBS II

What is the influence of a person (Man of Honor)? When you type that question into YourDictionary.com, here is the answer:

"Influence can be defined as the ability to affect the character, development, or behavior of someone or something, and it requires developing (a) strong emotional connection with yourself and others. Those who master the art of influence are often skilled at tapping into emotions that drive people('s) actions."

I write this chapter and dedicate this book to the men who have positively influenced and guided my character development. They have led with faith and integrity even through adversities as they pursued God and commitment to their families. And they have not only influenced me, but they have impacted the world.

The influence of man, either positive or negative, has written history. And the impact of a Man of Honor cannot be understated. Modeling integrity, forgiveness, leadership, spiritual responsibility, fathering sons, and showing how to love the women in their lives, both wives and daughters, can have ripple effects for generations. This chapter will touch on just some of the ways the men of my life have helped shape me to make me a better man, a man who honors well.

> Be watchful, stand firm in the faith, act like men (of honor), be strong. Let all that you do be in love. (1 Corinthians 16:13-14 ESV)

For as far back as I can remember, there have been four men who made such an impact on me: my father (whose namesake I carry), my grandfather (my dad's father), my other grandfather (my mom's father), and my stepfather (my mother's husband of 50+ years). All four have shaped my worldview, helped develop my character, and modeled leading with faith and integrity in most situations. But even when they did not model the best reactions or actions, they did model how to make things right, not by saying, "I am sorry," but by saying, "I was wrong, please forgive me." That was not easy, especially if they were angry or felt justified.

The men in my family are not perfect men, but they are forgiven men who learned to forgive and be forgiven. That character trait is why King David, an adulterer, murderer, and liar, could be called a man after God's heart. Because he knew how to make things right by asking for forgiveness and forgiving others. This lesson has stayed with me all my life, and I hope I continue to model this to my son, my grandchildren, and the men I have the privilege to lead and influence today.

Let me start with my mother's father, Pop C, as I always call him.

Pop C grew up in Philadelphia to two Italian immigrant parents and ran the streets as "Babo" in his teenage years until he was led to accept the Lord by his brother. He was on fire for God following his conversion to Christ, passionate and feeling called to be an evangelist. He went to Bible school and met my grandmother, Mom C, who also had a heart to share the Gospel. They married, started their ministry, then shortly thereafter, started their family. My mother was the first of their three children.

In the 1950s and 60s, through *The Voice of Healing,* my grandfather coordinated tent revivals and healing services across the United States and Cuba. After his crusade, he had such a heart for the Cuban people. He moved his family to Hollywood, Florida, so he could be a missionary and help the first Cuban refugees who came through the Freedom Tower in Miami following Castro's communist takeover. Through Pop C's obedience to this calling, God orchestrated my parents meeting at a youth group at Hollywood Assembly of God. Following your calling and having a heart for people always allows God to connect His people.

Pop C went on to start and lead many churches. He has walked with the Lord for over 82 years and has been an ordained minister for over 76 years. He still is my prayer warrior and spiritual mentor. Every night he prays, reads the Word, and worships. When I have stayed at his residence, I have heard his voice CRYING out to God in his bedroom late at night, calling out the names and needs of family members, friends, and ministries across the nation—in faith and fervency. What a powerful legacy!

My grandfather has always shown integrity, unwavering faith, love of family, and resilience following extreme adversity. Together with God, he has endured the tragic death of his grandson, the passing of his wife of 60+ years as he held her in his arms, financial and health challenges, child raising and family divorces, starting churches/ministries, and fallen ministers. Yet, he still teaches me to honor, love, and trust God always, even at 96 years old. His passion and faith are amazing to me. I hope I can have the same said of me when I am 96 - claiming 120!!!

. . . .

Now my other grandfather was Pop Hobbs. His first name was Jasper, like the precious stone mentioned in the Bible. Pop Hobbs was the most gentle, strong in character, and caring father and grandfather you could ever know. He was a Christian man and a true servant leader and was my rock when I was growing up. Pop Hobbs taught me my love for music, ice cream, and the water - boating, fishing, snorkeling, and adventure. He showed me that being "steady in the storm" is possible and modeled Christ-like unconditional love. He not only was my shelter while dealing with my two sets of divorced, opposite-personality parents, but he taught me to live life well. He modeled an exceptional work ethic and taught me what a strong silent man of honor is. Pop Hobbs shaped the man that I am and who I am becoming.

Jasper was not only Pop Hobbs to me; he was also my father's best friend. They would talk and debate for hours about being Christian, the end times, family dynamics, building churches, music, and giving of time and money. He supported my father in everything he did. He was the ultimate cheerleader.

Pop Hobbs was the assistant pastor for my dad in the church he started. He was in the construction industry and helped build and rebuild the church I grew up in. He gave selflessly and was extremely purpose-driven and mission-minded. I never saw him lose his temper. No matter how hurt or frustrated he got, he modeled assertive, loving, and directional interaction with people and family. Pop Hobbs and my father would say, "The jails are filled with men who cannot control their emotions, passion, or anger. Anyone can act and react on pure selfish emotions, but God has called us to be different, loving, kind, immovable, and forgiving. Because the relationship is always more important than the incident."

Pop Hobbs and my dad also taught me the true meaning of and how to forgive. "True forgiveness is when you can remember the hurt or incident and not feel the pain or emotions. While remembering, forgiveness allows me to separate the people from the emotions. Forgiving guilt, but withholding adjudication." I now know that is how our Lord loves and forgives us. I learned from their modeling. Pop Hobbs benefited from 200 years of Christian "man training." When we did his ancestry, we found six generations of Christian men who were leaders in faith, church, and family.

> Be kind to one another, tenderhearted, forgiving one another, even as God in Christ forgave you. (Ephesians 4:32 NKJV)

Tragically, Pop Hobbs was taken to heaven way too soon, when I was 14 years old. Even through the accident causing his death, Pop and my father showed me what being a man of God is. My father preached at his father's Christmas homegoing service, leading many to the Lord. After Pop Hobbs' death, financial issues surfaced. He had the wrong life insurance, a lack of savings, and was financially ignorant. This led my father to begin our financial coaching business in a crusade against the financial industry - a paradigm shift and defining moment for our family!

. . . .

The next man who has influenced my life is my stepfather. I have always called him Larry. Larry has been part of my life since I was three, and he married my mother when I was five. Larry never tried to be my father because I had a very present father. But he guided and modeled a completely different worldview, challenging me to think and act independently. Larry came from a non-practicing Jewish family and was forced to take responsibility at a young age due to the sudden death of his father. His mother did not work, and he had two young brothers at the time of his father's death. He strove for higher education and worked hard to help and support his mom and brothers. After college graduation and working for a few years in high-end sales, he made a change to become a government worker. And he married my mother.

The United States was in upheaval in the early 70s over the war in Vietnam, government crackdowns, and the rise of the hippie movement. The women's rights and the civil rights movements were in full swing. The hippie movement, led by the surge of baby boomers, was countercultural to the mainstream and religious ways of life, extolling the ideals of "free love" and "drugs, sex, and rock & roll." Larry and my mother gravitated toward this lifestyle, eventually leading them to move to Colombia, South America, for three years. That move impacted me as I felt abandoned by my mom at eight years old. I did not understand why they left, and I blamed Larry for taking my mother away, not knowing everything going on behind the scenes.

I lived with my father, who remarried when I was five years old. Shortly thereafter, he started a very conservative church for which I became the infamous "preacher's son." I will talk more about that later. I did not understand the dynamics of my parents' opposite worldviews, but the conflict and in-fighting affected me greatly, causing me to feel lost and act out negatively.

At eight years old, I was the problem preacher's son who felt abandoned by his hippie mother, who had left the country. I was trying to navigate the transition from being the only child that both of my parents pursued and fought for to being the lost child.

Despite the odds, the summer my mom left, I experienced one of my fondest childhood memories. Pop C and I traveled from Pennsylvania to California, zig-zagging the country in a motor home trek. With His strong, faithful influence, Pop C made an indelible mark on me. His guidance, coupled with the loving kindness of Pop Hobbs, got me through what could have been the worst year of my life. Those men of honor were powerful influences in my life. I can now understand that even Larry's different way of thinking helped guide and shape me to become the man I am today.

Larry and my mother returned from Colombia when I was 11. He went back to government work, they moved in with his mom for a short time, and I lived with them. I went from being the conservative preacher's son to the ex-hippie's child - a major metamorphosis. In their household, I was allowed and encouraged to be a free thinker and challenged to do and try different experiences at a young age. Larry was never a strong parental figure. He knew I had two parents with very strong personalities. More communicative than directive, he never lost a debate. Larry was always supportive and loved my mother, although they disagreed often. They had heated debates/arguments – yelling, screaming, and cursing to release emotions, then would return to each other's arms. It was quite different than anything I had ever experienced but reinforced what my father and grandfathers told me, "The relationship is always more important than the incident." Love never fails...

Through the years, I have seen Larry go through extreme adversities, including the tragic death of his only biological 2½-year-old son. Statistics show that up to 80% of marriages affected by the death of a child end in divorce[1], but Mom and Larry just celebrated 51 years of marriage and 54 years together. I also watched him experience the sudden deaths of his two younger brothers, care for his now 100-year-old mother, and become my mother's caretaker for the last ten years. Joyfully, I saw him get baptized and become a completed Jew shortly after my grandmother's sudden passing in 2005. He has loved my mother, he has loved my son, and he has loved me the best he knew how. He has been a dad whose perception and worldview, even though we do not agree on everything, have challenged me to look at people and this world differently. Because I had such diverse sets of parents, I can now relate to people from all backgrounds. If you can think and see the world from another's view, you can better relate to and influence them, making a difference in this world for the Kingdom. I love and thank him for that.

---

1   https://5littledoves.com

Now my father, to whom this book is dedicated and written in honor of.

Ken Senior was born and grew up in Hollywood, Florida. He was an only child, raised in a Christian home by God-loving parents, and involved in athletics, church, and church youth group. His dad, Pop Hobbs, loved and cherished his only son, instilled in him a good work ethic, and taught him how to honor and respect leaders in the church and positions of authority. Pop Hobbs taught my dad compassion for the lost and how to reach out to those in need, leading to a passion and desire to go into full-time ministry and business.

My father met my mother in youth group at church, and they were in the same grade at the same high school. My dad fell in love with this beautiful young evangelist's daughter, who was new to the area, school, and church. As I mentioned above, Pop Cerullo (her father) moved his family to Hollywood, Florida, to work with the first Cuban refugees. My dad gave my mom his class ring, and they went steady. After some time, my dad broke up with her, and she began talking and studying with a Jewish boy who lived a few houses down and went to the same school – his name was Larry. My mom fell in love with Larry, but dad was hooked and worked to win my mom back. He convinced my mom's father (Pop C – the evangelist) to persuade my mom to break up with Larry and to marry him instead, as he was going to Seminary and college. The plan worked, but you probably recognize the name Larry. Yes, the Jewish boy who lived a few houses down would later become my stepfather.

Pop C moved his family back to Philadelphia, Pennsylvania, and my dad and mom got married in September, just after they graduated high school and were starting college. My dad was 18, and my mom was 17. And I was conceived during their honeymoon just before my dad started his first year of college. I was born in July; that was the beginning of the end of their marriage.

My dad was highly convicted and passionate about his beliefs and pushed them on my mom, who rebelled because of her overly strict upbringing. I lived with Pop C on and off during my dad's four years in college. My father worked a job, worked at church, studied to get a degree, and had a wife and a child at 18 years old. Wow. I cannot even imagine the pressure all this had on my mom and dad's relationship. After my dad's college graduation, they tried to reconcile, moving back to Florida, but it did not last. I lived with my mom in a small apartment for a short time, but my dad wanted to have me with him as much as possible. They fought over me for years.

My father continued pursuing his calling to the ministry. He was a charismatic communicator and spoke at youth rallies across south Florida. He became a youth pastor and principal of a Christian school at a church in North Miami. When he spoke at a youth rally one night, a few girls from the young adult group from another church came to hear him. One of those girls met my dad and won his heart; she would become his wife, partner, and caretaker – and my stepmother – for over 50 years.

Because my mother worked many hours and had financial difficulties, I came to live with my dad earlier the same year he would remarry. My dad's mother (Mom Hobbs) was able to take a leave from her job to help care for me, and my mother agreed the change would be for the best. My dad's wedding was in September, and I was supposed to be in it. However, I was visiting my mother right before the wedding, and she did not bring me back in time, reinforcing the struggle between my mother and father.

The following year, my dad began his church on Mother's Day. Beginning in our home, the church eventually moved to the cafeteria of the school I attended. My father was purpose-driven, mission-minded, and consumed with growing the church and winning the lost.

I learned a lot from him during this time but didn't realize it until much later. He would get a school bus from a local glass company to pick up kids every Sunday for Sunday school and church. He had a "Defeat the Devil" campaign, where he had a friend dress in a devil costume and fly in on a helicopter at the Winn Dixie parking lot. He preached against the devil and shared the Gospel message, bringing many to the Lord. His passion and conviction walked the line between being purpose-driven and a workaholic. My dad loved people, and he loved to help people. He was a father to the fatherless and led the lost to Christ by being His hands and feet.

The defining moment in my dad's ministry at the church was when my grandfather, Pop Hobbs, was tragically killed in a car accident just before Christmas of 1979. My father preached the homegoing ceremony, but his ministry was not the same after.

A couple of years later, he was introduced to a company crusading to help families in America, working to right a wrong being done against them. He saw this business as a way to help families in the church gain control of their lives financially. I watched as his purpose-driven passion was reignited. My father left the ministry and became a lay pastor while he focused on building an amazing financial coaching business. He later mentored two of my brothers and me, and we joined him as business partners. When he passed away in 2021, he had built ten brokerages, had over 10,000 clients, over 300 licensed representatives across the country, and over $160 Million in assets managed. I am honored to continue his legacy of helping families for the benefit of our family.

My father was not a perfect man, husband, or father. But he was a perfectly forgiven man, husband, and father. He mentored, pursued, encouraged, and modeled servant leadership, and he loved me truly, deeply, and completely the best he could. He was an amazing grandfather to his ten grandchildren and a surrogate father to many other men. He became all of the best attributes of his own father. He taught me to love unconditionally and pursue family and people for the Lord and relationship. He taught me that even if you have not been a good father, husband, or child, you can fix the wounds with a relentless pursuit of love, forgiveness, and relationship. Faults can be forgiven, and restoration is always possible if you mirror our Lord in Revelation 3:19-21. My father did this until the end. I know he is sitting and talking to Jesus about his sons and family every day.

All those I love; I unmask and train. So repent and be eager to pursue what is right. Behold I'm standing at the door, knocking... If your heart is open to hear my voice and you open the door within, I will come in to you and feast with you. And to the one who conquers I will give you the privilege of sitting with me on my throne. (Revelation 3:19-21 TPT)

These four men have influenced my life and the lives of thousands. The impact of a man has great rewards.

Have you thought about who you are influencing in your life? You can influence your family and others to be Men of Honor for generations to come. We all experience adversity. But we can all overcome any adversity with faith in God and action on that faith. Remember...

"Influence can be defined as the ability to affect the character, development, or behavior of someone or something, and it requires developing strong emotional connection with yourself and others. Those who master the art of influence are often skilled at tapping into emotions that drive people's actions."

Influence, good or bad, has changed the world throughout history. And the influence we each exhibit will steer the future. The influence of these men has molded me to become a leader, an overcomer, an entrepreneur in business and ministry, and a better husband, child, and father. The support and wisdom they have poured out have guided me throughout my life, and more recently, my involvement with 5+ para-church ministries. In the last 10 years alone, I've started or worked with men's bootcamps and coaching, women leadership and empowerment, orphan care and education, financial coaching and business/not-for-profit training, and healing encounter events.

One of my most significant areas of influence is working with the Band of Brothers Bootcamps. This endeavor has highly impacted over 10,000 men as they teach aspects of forgiveness and "man training" with cool, healing, manly activities that draw participants in.

One thing for sure is that as we grow, we are called to influence others. We each have a responsibility to take our place in history. No matter your past or who has influenced you, you are an influencer – make sure you leave a *good* legacy.

Here are some steps you can take:

- Visit www.unitedmenofhonor.com and find a Bootcamp you can attend.

- Encourage the women in your life to get involved at www.womenworldleaders.com

- See how you can be instrumental in education and caring for orphans at www.Kerusglobal.org

- Go to www.PRImerica.com/kenhobbs2 for financial coaching and business coaching.

- Visit www.HealingEncounterNights.com to find out how you can participate in an upcoming Healing Encounter event.

My prayer is that all men who are led by God will step out in faith and conquer any adversity they have faced or are facing now with the Blood of the Lamb, the Word of their testimony, and the power of God working in them. You can be that Man of Honor and the Man of Influence that this world so desperately needs.

They conquered him completely through the blood of the Lamb and the powerful word of his testimony. They triumphed because they did not love and cling to their own lives, even when faced with death. (Revelation 12:11-12 TPT)

Join me. Armor up and prepare to be "fit to fight" as we charge through this world, equipped with the whole armor of God, as United Men of Honor.

FAITH TO OVERCOME ABANDONMENT

Suffering from the fear of abandonment is an overwhelming worry that consumes you when you feel that people who are close to you will leave. There are many reasons for this fear, and even believers and the strongest men can be affected.

Abandonment issues can arise when someone gets treated poorly or even left by someone significant. When this occurs multiple times, fear and distrust of others are reinforced. Death, divorce, and trauma may bring feelings of neglect, isolation, and abandonment. Being left by someone you love can be devastating and debilitating, creating a serious emotional crisis that can crush your self-esteem as you are cut off from a vital relationship in your life.

God can soothe this deep pain as we allow Him to heal and strengthen us. However, it is our choice to allow Him to heal us.

I personally must work to overcome my own fear of abandonment, and I believe more people struggle with this issue than we realize. Attempting to deal with the fear, sometimes I press in toward a friendship or a relationship and try hard to make someone happy until I am left exhausted and empty. Other times, I put up a wall around myself to avoid getting hurt further. Neither option is healthy. So instead, I've learned to release my fear to God.

Healing from abandonment comes for me when I can peel back layer upon layer with God and walk through it with Him. I have a checklist

I can go through that helps keep me on track. I am only offering my advice as a man of honor, hoping this may trigger a way for you to be aware when this happens to you. I am not a counselor or a therapist, just a man who goes before God for my help in this area. Here are some things that God has taught me:

SET BOUNDARIES. The first thing I've learned to do is to set boundaries. When we rely on our faith and follow God's guidance for setting boundaries, He will remind us of our self-worth. God alone can help you stop the negative thinking process and input new thoughts in your spirit such as: *Not everyone wants to leave you. You are not disposable; you are God's creation!*

TRUST WHAT GOD SAYS. Trusting what God says will allow you to accept the truth of the abandonment wound, show yourself grace and love, and validate the wounds that abandonment has created in your life. Accept that there is a purpose for the pain you feel. God never dismisses any harm that is done to you. Talk to Him about it in prayer.

ADMIT YOUR STRUGGLE. When I admit my struggle with abandonment, it releases my shame and guilt. I am human, and I have been deeply hurt; that does not make me inadequate or weak. Shame and guilt are liars! Staying stuck in self-pity blocks healing and breakthrough.

LOVE YOURSELF THE WAY GOD LOVES YOU. Ask God how to restore yourself and restore what has been stolen so you can receive His radical grace, mercy, and healing love.

> *Can a mother forget the baby at her breast and have no compassion on the child she has borne? Though she may forget, I will not forget you! See, I have engraved you on the palms of my hands; your walls are ever before me.* (Isaiah 49:15-16 NIV)

God will NEVER leave you! God will never leave me. Let's say these affirmations and quote truth from His Word because His promises are true. We can look to our heavenly Father to help us and prosper us. He will show His favor toward His sons.

> *Be strong and courageous. Do not be afraid; do not be discouraged, for the Lord your God will be with you wherever you go.* (Joshua 1:9 NIV)

GUY SHASHATY

Guy Shashaty was born and raised in South Florida with six brothers and sisters. He attended Hialeah-Miami Lakes (HML) Sr. high school.

Upon graduating from Liberty University in Lynchburg, Virginia, where Guy played football, he returned to South Florida, where he was a coach and teacher for eight years.

In 1988 Guy was introduced to the financial services business. At the time, he was working seven part-time jobs at the school to make extra money. He worked the business part-time for 3.5 years before going full-time in June 1991.

Guy has spent the last 34 years recruiting and training thousands of people to become successful in business. They now have 130 Regional Vice President offices and 9,000 financial representatives.

Guy leads the Band of Brothers, a men's ministry in Florida that is transforming men and helping them find the answers to their most pressing questions.

Guy married his wife Kathy in December of 1989. He has three sons—Javan, Asher, and Tiras—a daughter-in-law—Melissa, and 3 grandchildren—Elijah, Kara, and Truett.

NOT THE SHARPEST TOOL IN THE SHED

BY COACH GUY SHASHATY

I was born and raised in a 975-square-foot home with nine people, including my four older sisters, two younger brothers, and my parents. My childhood was awesome when it included sports.

When I was in the 3rd grade, there was a test that the school I attended gave in the evening. One night, all the students in my class had to return to school. The test occurred in the cafeteria, with many other students and parents milling around.

The instructor placed a piece of paper in front of me with a rectangle, square, and triangle all intersecting. The instructions were simply to draw that same picture on a blank piece of paper. I could easily draw a rectangle, square, or triangle, but these were all intersecting, and for some reason, I could not do it. I remember the instructor trying to help me understand the assignment. I understood what I was supposed to do, but I couldn't do it.

From a distance, I noticed the instructor talking to my parents and them looking back at me. I instantly felt uneasy. On the ride home, it was silent in the car. Finally, my mom broke the silence by asking me a question. "So, you couldn't draw that diagram?"

I instantly said, "No!!"

From that day on, my parents were the most encouraging, loving, and supportive people regarding anything I had to do with sports. But when it came to the classroom, I always felt they were hoping I would somehow just get by.

I was *that* kid - the one who could not sit still and was disruptive and constantly distracted. This caused many issues for me. I was labeled a "problem child." From the 3rd grade to the 10th grade, I was regularly disciplined. I knew studying and staying focused was not my thing, and my parents never pushed me. They accepted that the classroom was always going to be tough for me.

Sports were different. I excelled at a high level in both baseball and football. My escape was the field. That was where I made the honor roll. My grades suffered - I would get C's, D's, and occasionally an F. Somehow, I managed to get by until I entered high school. Then I was told by my football coach that to play sports, I needed a 2.0 grade point average. My GPA was 1.7 at the time. I remember deciding that night that I was going to do whatever was necessary to get to 2.0. I focused for the first time in the classroom like I did on the field.

Around that time, I was invited by Johnny Thomas, a running back on the football team, to go to a Fellowship of Christian Athletes (FCA) meeting. I asked him what that was. He told me it was a club where athletes get together to discuss the challenges that athletes go through and how to overcome them. So, I started attending FCA meetings weekly. That summer, I was invited to an FCA Camp in Black Mountain, North Carolina. I went because there were going to be professional football players there who I could learn from. Throughout the week, there were meetings where these professional athletes told their stories. The stories were similar in many ways. The athletes had money, possessions, and women - pretty much whatever they wanted. But they all said it left them empty, and it wasn't until they accepted Jesus Christ into their lives that the empty void was finally filled. They now had peace, joy, and fulfillment.

I grew up believing everything they were talking about. I went to a Catholic school from 1st – 8th grade, where I learned all about Jesus. I knew all the stories. I already believed that. But by the end of the week, I felt uneasy about what I was hearing.

The leader of my group pulled me aside and asked me some questions. He said, "Guy, if you died tonight would you go to heaven?"

I said, "Yes. I grew up Catholic and went to Catholic school. I was even an altar boy for four years." I took my beliefs seriously and knew I was going to heaven.

He said, "It sounds like you have head knowledge, but do you have heart knowledge?"

I was confused by that, and he explained that many people believe in God intellectually, but have never accepted Jesus into their life, have never asked for forgiveness, and have never turned away from their old life.

Then he pulled out his Bible and showed me Romans 3:23, where it says that *All have sinned and fall short of the glory of God.* (NIV) I told him I agreed that I was a sinner.

He then showed me Romans 6:23, *For the wages of sin is death, but the gift of God is eternal life in Christ Jesus our Lord.* (NIV) He asked me if I had ever accepted that gift. I said no.

He then took me to Romans 10:9, where it says, *If you declare with your mouth "Jesus is Lord" and believe in your heart that God raised him from the dead, you will be saved.* (NIV) He asked me if I wanted to accept Jesus into my heart and know for sure that I would go to heaven. I said yes and prayed to receive Jesus that night in June of 1978.

Everything after that was different. I read my Bible and prayed every day, and hung out with other believers. I was learning and growing. As a result, God taught me new things. I had decided in my head that I was "not the sharpest tool in the shed." I believed that most people were just smarter than I was – that my edge was on the field, and I would never excel in the classroom.

Then I read in Genesis 1:27 that we are *made in the image of God.* (NIV) I remember thinking that if I am made in God's image, there is nothing I can't do. So, I canceled the agreement I had made in my head and, literally overnight, became one of the smartest people I knew. My new perspective and belief about life and what I am capable of have propelled me ever since. I graduated in the top 10% of my class with a 3.2 GPA, received a full football scholarship to Liberty University, graduated four years later, and began my career as a teacher in Miami-Dade County, Florida. While teaching and coaching, I went to school at night and got my master's degree. At every school I taught, I ran FCA huddles. I loved teaching and coaching and never thought I would do anything else.

Even though I loved my job, my finances were a mess. I was making $31,000 a year to teach. And I had seven part-time jobs at the school that paid me an extra $9,000 a year. How could someone have seven part-time jobs? I coached baseball and football ($1,500), taught an extra class every day ($2,000), sponsored a club ($450), taught night school ($1,000), taught (begged for) summer school ($1,050), and earning my master's degree paid me an extra $3,000 a year. Still, every year I spent more money than I made. I had $23,000 in credit card debt at age 25. I was the guy that went to school every day with shorts, a t-shirt, sneakers, a hat, and a whistle around my neck. I'm sure you remember "that coach" at your school. I was made for this job and never dreamed I would do anything else. But God had other plans.

In 1988, I was introduced to an opportunity to make extra money in financial services. If you knew me, that would be the last thing you would think I would ever do. I was a coach and teacher, not a financial advisor. But it was proposed to me that I could eliminate all or some of my part-time jobs while working a flexible schedule. So I decided to give it a shot.

Through this new endeavor, I learned so many valuable concepts that I knew everyone needed to know. The founder of the company, Art Williams, was a former football coach. He was the most motivating man I had ever met and was speaking my language. I did the business part-time for 3.5 years before deciding to go full-time. My disenchantment with the school system was growing worse, and I knew I wanted to be my own boss, call my own shots, and give options and choices to my family, but I was struggling with whether this was where God wanted me.

Fortunately, in December of 1989, I married Kathy, the love of my life. I came home one day and was obviously bothered by whether to leave teaching and coaching. Kathy simply said, "Do you really want to be a coach your whole life?" That was the day I realized how she felt about my chosen profession and that she saw more in me than what I saw in myself.

So, in June of 1991, I left teaching and coaching to go into financial services full-time. I took with me the belief that I was made in the image of God (Gen. 1:27), and there was nothing I couldn't do. I also knew that God had gifted me with a tremendous work ethic, organization and administrative skills, leadership, and a burning desire to do something special with my life.

I remember getting my master's degree and thinking how happy I was that I would not have to read another book as long as I lived. Boy, that was a stupid thought!! Since changing direction and going into financial services, I have read thousands of books, including biographies of successful people, leadership books, and personal development books. You name it; if it would help me grow my business, I was all in.

My new career allowed me to recruit and train new people in the business. I was surprised to learn how few people were confident and how little many believed in themselves. Many were professing Christians, yet had not embraced that they were made in the image of God, enabling them to move forward in life and tackle anything with confidence. Helping others recognize that God does not make junk and He will get us through any challenge became my calling.

My focus had switched from teaching the team about financial services to teaching the team about winning and what it took to be successful. Life is challenging. Nobody escapes adversity. But, if you are where God wants you to be and you put your head down and go to work with the right heart, eventually, the blessings will begin to happen. I've never met anyone successful who didn't have to break bad internal agreements and get rid of limiting beliefs about themselves and others.

That was the attitude that proved to be successful. Today, our business continues to grow. We currently have 130 offices and over 9,000 financial advisors. Not bad for a guy who believed he was "not the sharpest tool in the shed."

I am also leading a men's ministry called the Band of Brothers. We help men figure it out. We help them become the man God created them to be. As a result, thousands have come to Christ, been discipled, and given the tools to "go" and do the same for other men.

Along the way, several people have had a tremendous impact on my life, and I would like to thank them. First, my wife has been supportive from the start. She has great discernment and follows behind me to heal the damage I do unknowingly to people I thought I was motivating. She has proven to be a vital asset in our business; we would not have the success we have without her. Second, Johnny Thomas for having the courage to face possible rejection and introduce me to Jesus Christ. Third, pastor John Macarthur, who discipled me when I became a Christian. I would listen to him on the radio every night while going to sleep. Even to this day, I follow him closely and have been so blessed by his steadfastness, integrity, and willingness to tell the truth. Fourth, Art Williams changed the direction of my life. I was on my way to a life of mediocrity, and he came along and shook me up, cleaned out the toxins in my brain, and gave me the confidence to break ties with the past. Fifth, Greg Fitzpatrick, my mentor and the person I go to for advice and counsel in my business. Thank you for being there for us. There are many more teammates that have had a positive impact on our business. Thank you to all of them.

In conclusion, I want to leave you with a few absolute truths.

1. The only way to fill your void or emptiness is with Jesus Christ. There is no other way. In John 14:6 Jesus says, *"I am the way, the truth, and the life. No one comes to the father except through me."* (NIV) God has a plan for your life. You can figure out that plan through prayer, reading his Word, and possibly fasting. Then put blinders on, keep your head down and go to work with everything you got. The world is full of naysayers and mediocre people - that's what the blinders are for.

2. Find coaches and mentors to counsel you along the way. Make sure they are people who have traveled the road you are on and can give you the advice you need.

3. We are just passing through this life. If you are blessed, you have about 80 years to make the impact you were created for. Stop wasting time. Trust God and get after it. Go all in!!!

4. Your ultimate purpose here on earth is to love the Lord your God with all your heart, mind, and body. (Matthew 22:37)

5. Your second purpose is to go and make disciples. (Matthew 28:19)

The most effective way to live out your purpose is to gain influence. You gain influence by being successful. Get great at what God has called you to do, and people will listen and follow. When people need answers, they don't seek counsel from unsuccessful people or from average and ordinary people. Instead, they seek it from people with influence, those who have done or are doing great things.

God Bless You.

Now, go do great things!!!

Coach Guy

FAITH TO OVERCOME INSECURITIES

There are many causes of insecurity, but chief among them is our failure to fully trust God. Jeremiah 17:7-8 (NKJV) teaches us,

Blessed is the man who trusts in the Lord,
And whose hope is in the Lord,
For he shall be like a tree planted by the waters,
Which spreads out its roots by the river,
And will not fear when heat comes,
But its leaves will be green,
And will not be anxious in the year of drought,
Nor will it cease from yielding fruit.

God made us to love Him, others, and ourselves and to put our trust and hope in Him alone. One of the causes of insecurity is that we become preoccupied with ourselves and put our hope in what others think of us. When we focus on ourselves, we do not love God or others as we were created to; we don't put God on His throne or appreciate and enjoy the masterpiece that He created others to be. Philippians 2:3 tells us we should not do anything from selfish ambition or conceit, but in humility, we are to count others more significant than ourselves.

Another cause of insecurity is relying on our wealth, possessions, and accomplishments to determine our identity. From an early age, society grooms us to attach our self-worth to things and achievements instead of recognizing our value as God's children. So, as we navigate a culture that strongly emphasizes what we do and always encourages us to be Number One, how are we supposed to handle the paralyzing insecurities that come from not measuring up? When we are insecure, we reveal that we are longing for justification from people rather than recognizing our worth in God. God richly provides everything for us to enjoy (1 Timothy 6:17), and He wants us to trust Him.

God loves you just the way you are. He created you with all your "manhood" and attributes. Insecurities can come when we are preoccupied paying attention to the "securities" of this world and what those securities deem as important. We will never obtain them all. We can tackle these by searching God's Word to find where we put our priorities, but first, we must know the truth about our identity as men of God before we can combat insecurities elsewhere.

Our obedience with a right heart is what pleases the Lord; unfortunately, many of us get hung up on having a better reputation with people than with God. We seek to emulate others and, at times, become overly obsessive when we long for validation and respect from people or accolades from our career to boost our worthiness. We forsake the righteousness of Christ that makes us worthy. (Romans 6:17) If we know that we were created in the image of God, as the Bible says (Genesis 1:27), then when we give our lives to Christ, we are no longer defined by our past since we are now a new creation. (2 Corinthians 5:17)

It takes faith to overcome our insecurities. Just as the Apostle Paul said, *I count everything as lost because of the surpassing worth of knowing Christ Jesus my Lord.* (Philippians 3:7-8 ESV) In knowing Christ, we are no longer condemned, we are God's workmanship, and we know we were fearfully designed in the womb, wonderfully made by our magnificent Creator. We are chosen and redeemed, and we are the work of God's hands. We are the sons of God—His heirs.

Insecurity as a "status" was never God's will for your life. So do not make it one. God has called you to look to Him alone for your source of security. Do not doubt your security in Christ, giving Satan the win. God is in control, and His sovereignty extends to anyone who believes in His Son, Jesus Christ.

True security will come when you recognize that God will supply every need of yours according to His riches and glory in Jesus Christ. (Philippians 4:19) God and His Word are unchanging, and although we live in a physical world, we are reminded that *our struggle is not against flesh and blood.* (Ephesians 6:12 NIV) We are in a constant fight with the enemy of our souls. Christ paid a tremendous price to purchase our salvation and break us free from bondage. Insecurity is a prison we choose to put ourselves in.

God will give you the strength by faith as you trust Him to overcome insecurity. Never forget God's promise to keep you in His perfect peace when your mind is steadfast because you trust Him. (Isaiah 26:3) It is such a comfort to know peace and that the God of your inner peace gives you every affirmation in His Word that you are loved, just the way He created you.

You've got what it takes!

. . . .

JIM SAYIH

Jim Sayih has dedicated his life to service. He is a service-oriented advocate leader helping those with disabilities navigate life towards independence through inclusion. Currently, he serves as Executive Director of Special Compass, a non-profit 501-C-3 organization serving those who are "Differently Abled."

Jim's life of service began as a young, newly saved Christian stationed in Japan. When he returned to the United States, he began a ministry in South Florida— visiting the jails in Miami and giving Bible studies to inmates.

Jim is a 10-year Air Force veteran and retired Police Lieutenant with multiple commendations who relies on his faith and utilizes his Master's of Science in Exercise and Sports Science to help others. Having co-authored the best-selling book *The Success Secret* and leading and implementing many events aimed at furthering his goal of inclusion for all, Jim has been featured on *Good Morning America,* multiple news outlets, *Muscle & Fitness* magazine, and several local and national newspapers.

To learn more, visit www.SpecialCompass.Org or reach out to Jim at Jim@SpecialCompass.Org

DIFFERENTLY ABLED

BY JIM SAYIH

She was bleeding, pregnant for just 28 weeks when Michael was surgically removed from his mother and entered this world. Michael weighed 3.8 pounds and was hospitalized for ten days before he began to feed, cry, and strive like any newborn. Six weeks later, he got an ear infection. So I drove my precious son to Joe DiMaggio Hospital, not the same hospital of his birth, beginning a journey that would grow my faith.

After an overnight stay and multiple tests, including a cat scan, the neurologist met with me to discuss Michael's diagnosis. The doctor sketched Michael's brain on a napkin, then shaded in all the areas of his brain damage. I asked, "Did you say brain damage?"

She replied, "Yes, severe brain damage."

"From an ear infection?" I questioned.

Before she answered, the neurologist wanted to know about Michael's birth. I learned that his mom's bleeding had resulted from the placenta tearing away from the uterus - something doctors call an abruption. This condition deprived Michael of blood and oxygen until he was delivered, causing much of his brain tissue to die. That neurologist brought in two more neurologists to explain Michael's etiological future. All three recommended that I place Michael in an institution because he would require full-time care, ending my freedom.

I remained silent until they all offered their recommendations. The room was quiet after the last one spoke. I was staring at the floor during that time. Then, I remember looking up for a few seconds, taking a deep breath, glancing into each set of eyes, and saying, "Michael will live a life filled with abundance, and he will be included in everything."

They all said good luck. And left. We were discharged shortly thereafter.

> *"Have I not commanded you? Be strong and courageous. Do not be afraid; do not be discouraged, for the LORD your God will be with you wherever you go."* (Joshua 1:9 NIV)

The drive home from the hospital with Michael was quiet. I visualized how he would develop and, simultaneously, was emotionally shocked, asking God, "How can this be?" I knew explaining this to Michael's mother was going to be traumatic. All my years of law enforcement training and experience had not prepared me enough for this. I was not sure if she would want to follow the neurologists' recommendations or my decision.

As expected, the news crushed Michael's mother. Just one year previous, on the same date, Michael's brother Adam was born, weighing 10 pounds. I told her this wasn't her fault and that we would include Michael in everything, no matter how challenging. I prayed for God to help me manage this new, unexpected, lifelong commitment. A helpless mindset clouded my head, but Jesus seemed to hold my hand, reassuring me that good would come.

> And we know that for those who love God all things work together for good, for those who are called according to his purpose. (Romans 8:28 ESV)

I prayed relentlessly for Michael's healing, but I didn't see any miracles I hoped for. Then, I went through a period of anger at God, thinking, *How could God let this happen?* Heart-pounding pain enveloped me as I looked at my tiny, helpless, dependent son entering a world filled with uncertainty. My control here was very limited, and the unknown was causing a ton of fear. Fear like I've never experienced. It seemed like I was being forced to have faith; there was no other option.

> Fear not, for I am with you; be not dismayed, for I am your God. I will strengthen you, I will help you, I will uphold you with my righteous right hand. (Isaiah 41:10 ESV)

"Where do people like Michael go for help?" became my preamble in most conversations. Finally, I found a place in Philadelphia called The Institutes for the Achievement of Human Potential. I spent ten days there with Michael, learning about home therapies. His therapy would require 8-12 hours daily, seven days a week. We converted our home into a therapy studio, and volunteers would help on an hourly basis. We developed a small community of people who loved Michael and believed in our mission to help improve his abilities.

> *Carry each other's burdens, and in this way you will fulfill the law of Christ. (Galatians 6:2 NIV)*

Five years later, I asked Michael if he wanted to participate in a duathlon race, which included a five-kilometer run, a 30-kilometer bike leg, and another five-kilometer run. I told him his brother Adam would join us, and Michael immediately said yes. For the run, Michael stayed in his stroller while I pushed. For the bike, I attached a framed partial bike and strapped in his torso. We encountered a couple of wrecks and equipment failures, but we finished the run, crossing the finish line. Adam was waiting for us. Michael was beaming with joy, proudly wearing his finisher medal. Soon after, another race was announced, and Michael wanted to enter. I agreed, even though many people harshly judged me, saying that it was too dangerous, especially since we experienced equipment problems and crashes. But I knew this was something God had called us to.

> *I have fought the good fight, I have finished the race, I have kept the faith. (2 Timothy 4:7 NIV)*

So, we planned for the next race, crossed the finish line, and again that same face of joy and fulfillment burst forth. Not only did Michael love these races and listening to people screaming his name, but spectators who witnessed his joy were impacted and inspired.

Other parents quickly learned about what we were doing; some would ask if I would tow their kid at a race. My response was, "If I take your child, then Michael will be a spectator." So instead, I recruited friends who were runners, asking if they would tow these kids.

Unfortunately, Michael's mother did not support our endeavor, and we soon got a divorce. I was awarded full custody of both Michael and Adam. My biggest concern in raising the boys was ensuring I balanced time for Adam, as Michael received so much attention due to his needs. Sometimes I would walk into their room, lay on their bed, and say nothing; just lay there quietly. They would look at me and say, "What are you doing, Dad?" Other times they would ignore me. But I made it a priority to be present and not let a day go by for either of them without being noticed. At times God would nudge my heart, reminding me to not go to bed yet; but to go to their room. Thank God!

> Start children off on the way they should go, and even when they are old they will not turn from it. (Proverbs 22:6: NIV)

School had its own challenges for Michael. I thought all teachers would consider his best interest and support him as I did, but my frustration became almost routine when managing his school needs, rights, and eligibilities. School administrators tried to manipulate our goals with the same limited mentality as the doctors who recommended an institution. The struggles of including Michael in activities with others angered me, as I witnessed parents pretend to be sympathetic but avoid lending a helping hand. It hurt to watch Michael be alone while others developed friendships and did not include Michael. Occasionally, an angel kid would come into Michael's life as a genuine friend. You could see Michael light up with life when a friend called or asked him to go to a movie or a game. The problem was that Michael didn't know how to manage friendships. If a friend stopped seeing him, depression would set in. I would pray for his growth, knowing that more relationship hurdles would be ahead. Trusting God to help me with Michael was challenging. Thoughts of how unfair his life was compared to others surfaced. Then I would think about others who have it worse than Michael, and I would be grateful for his abilities.

After graduation, Michael got a job with the Miami Dolphins as a greeter. At first, I would step back and watch how he would interact with fans coming through the door. Sometimes I wanted to defend him against some customers, but I had to control myself and let him experience it for himself. This was very hard for me, very hard. I had to trust God to guide Michael. Then, after a couple of years, he got a promotion. At the Super Bowl, Michael was awarded a Gold Helmet for Outstanding Customer Service.

> *His master said to him, 'Well done, good and faithful servant. You have been faithful over a little; I will set you over much. Enter into the joy of your master.'* (Matthew 25:21 ESV)

In 2015, the Lord touched my heart to create Special Compass, a nonprofit 501(c)3, to serve those with physical disabilities. Michael is the

President, and I am the Executive Director. Nobody receives a salary. We are all 100% volunteers. Michael had been racing in events since he was 5 years old. Now, our goal was to give this experience to others like Michael, helping them with friendships, employment, housing, education, and ultimately, independence. I wasn't sure if God wanted us to do this, but the more we served, the more blessings we saw.

Everybody has challenges. Everybody. When our volunteers help our Differently Abled athletes cross a finish line, the Abled-bodied athlete is equally fulfilled, knowing that it was their arms and legs that served to propel their Buddy to experience crossing the finish line. I thought my personal friends would support, sponsor and encourage me in this journey, but I soon learned that our mission attracted new friends, allowing us to develop a community of like-minded, faithful, service-oriented people. Still, God is teaching me that not everybody will be sympathetic to our mission, but I can slow down and allow Him to manage the time and resources necessary to execute His plans. And just when I think He is not listening, God shows off His divine plan as only He can do. I'm constantly humbled by His love and reminded that He works all things for good, including Michael's brain injury. Never would I have thought that all our adversities would have brought us to where we are today.

> *Now to him who is able to do far more abundantly than all that we ask or think, according to the power at work within us. (Ephesians 3:20 ESV)*

In 2017, the Lord touched my heart to build an adaptive apartment complex for people with disabilities. This is not my field, but I proposed to Special Compass that we build the apartment for the Differently Abled.

Michael said to me, "Dad, you don't know how to do that."

"You're right, but I believe the Lord wants us to do this," I answered.

We started searching for land and came up empty. So, I began to assemble a building committee, which took two years. I asked God to attract genuine talent that would serve our interests. Today we have 12 talented, experienced members. These are people I would not normally associate with but are now my friends and trusted advisors. Still, we did not find land on which to build. Becoming impatient, I started to doubt. But somehow, my faith would get recharged with small milestones of progress that only God could provide.

> Don't worry about tomorrow, for tomorrow will bring its own worries. Today's trouble is enough for today. (Matthew 6:34 NLT)

Then, during COVID, Michael and I visited a married couple who both use wheelchairs. They gave us a tour of their home and shared their dream of home improvements. When we returned home, Michael asked me if we could make their home improvement dream come true. I answered, "Let's see."

One week later, God provided a plan, sponsors, and volunteers. Again, this is not my field. God provided a new air conditioner and enabled us to expand their master bedroom. Additionally, we built a fence around the house and added a patio. We tiled the new bedroom and added two new walls, three new doors, a new window, and new ceilings. We painted the interior and exterior and added new lighting and sprinklers. This project was all God. It cost the owners of the home nothing, and the people who volunteered were fulfilled as they served. This Adaptive Home Makeover event made the front page of the Sun Sentinel. Two weeks later, I received a call from the city manager in Pembroke Pines to discuss a land opportunity for our apartment project.

> And my God will supply every need of yours according to his riches in glory in Christ Jesus. (Philippians 4:19 ESV)

The day of the land site visit was incredible. As I drove past a parcel near my scheduled meeting, I openly voiced in the privacy of my truck, "Boy, wouldn't it be great if that was the parcel I'm scheduled to see?"

Minutes later, I met the city manager, who led me to the lot I had just driven by, saying, "What do you think?"

I was shocked and told him what I had said to myself when I drove past earlier. Everybody laughed and acknowledged what we all knew: God had managed it. Faith in letting God manage our efforts was manifesting itself before my eyes. God's timing is always perfect. If the city manager had presented this opportunity two years earlier, I would not have been ready to execute God's plan; but those two years had allowed us to form the building committee, setting us up for the moment. Thank God for orchestrating this whole process. Each step of the way, God has faithfully come through and masterfully placed all the right pieces in place.

Meanwhile, Michael was watching how God made this happen, knowing that my skill set was not in construction and development. He witnessed God bring the experts we needed by faith, and even using adversity. God moved people, events, circumstances, and money to align the way He intended to reveal His goodness and purpose.

> *You are the God who works wonders; you have made known your might among the peoples. (Psalm 77:14: ESV)*

Looking back at all the pain, adversity, and lessons God allowed is incredible. If someone had told me that my life would be better and that together, my son and I would impact others, I would not have believed them. Yet, the friendships we have today are a direct result of our adversities and triumphs. And those we serve benefit from our experiences, good and not so good.

Our unexpected journeys have developed our faith and continue to teach us to embrace our growth and God's timing. And as I watch fellow believers exercise their faith, God continues to strengthen my understanding of how He uses people at any skill level to successfully accomplish His work. So I can wait patiently, watch Him with confidence, and work diligently to make all things happen for His glory. God leads and believes in us all. The key is to let Him lead.

> *Trust in the Lord with all your heart, and do not lean on your own understanding. In all your ways acknowledge him, and he will make straight your paths. (Proverbs 3:5-6 ESV)*

Being a parent of a Differently Abled person requires a willingness to share oneself indefinitely. It requires constant time management. But every traumatic chapter in my life has had a meaningful purpose that God has faithfully sculpted, and I am grateful for the pain that has made me the man of faith I am today. We can trust that God will use our discomfort, giving us faith to improve so that we can serve others with grace and humility. He certainly knows what He is doing. I wish I had known this in my teen years, but I now realize I needed the pain allowed me to develop into a Man of Honor. I appreciate God's wisdom, and I love Him for loving me, loving those I serve, and loving humanity.

Amen!

Jim Sayih

LEE SHIPP

Pastor Lee Shipp, as the founder and senior pastor of First New Testament Church, has ministered God's Word through the power of the Holy Spirit for over thirty-six years. Led by a devotion to his Savior and a love for the scriptures, God has used him to teach and preach throughout the world through conferences, camp meetings, and revivals. Pastor Shipp is also founder and President of "A Call To The Heart," a ministry of evangelism and outreach through radio, television, literature, and national and international campaigns. Pastor Shipp also serves on the boards of Adullam International Ministries, All For Christ International, Changed By the Glory Ministries, and East Harlem Fellowship. Pastor Shipp and his family live in Baton Rouge, Louisiana, where they continue to serve the Lord with their church family.

Pastor Shipp can be reached at www.fntchurch.org or 225-293-2222.

LEAVE IT IN GETHSEMANE

BY LEE SHIPP

Gethsemane is the place to cry. It is the place for agony. It is where we sweat and plead with God. There, in Gethsemane, is where we can say, "No! Lord, is there not another way?" In Gethsemane, Jesus the Son of God cried and pled for another way. In this garden, you can shrink back from the fear. You can protest the coming pain. This is the garden where Christians don't always have to fake a smile and pretend they have it all together.

I lived in my Gethsemane for three and a half years before God would take me to the event of my crucifixion: the epic moment of betrayal, deceit, and abandonment. It was in Gethsemane that the Lord would teach me how to die, how to face the event so I could live again when it was all over. I am convinced that had it not been for my Gethsemane, I would have died in my affliction.

Many are under the impression that Christians should not expose their hurts. They feel that Christians should not voice their contempt for injustice. Instead, Christians should just smile and bear all the abuse without making any appeal. However, that reasoning is false. God gives us a place where we can cry and pour out our complaints, a place where we can express our pain over the way we have been treated or the injustice we have suffered. Men of honor suffer. Men of honor cry. Men of honor have a Gethsemane – a place where they can "gut it out."

Gethsemane is a place where we question the afflictions of life. Gethsemane is the place where you can point out your fears and even beg God for a different course. You don't have to fake it. To be a man of honor, you don't have to pretend you are ok. You don't have to hide the pain and the fears.

You have a place where you can cry and plead, a place where you can hurt and expose your wounds. For Job, Gethsemane was sitting on top of his pile of ashes while he beheld the utter devastation of his life and family. For Jeremiah, Gethsemane was a prison cell where he gutted out the book of Lamentations. For David, it was the secret place where his songs poured out to God. For Jesus, Gethsemane was a garden, a quiet spot where He often retreated to be with His Father. For many believers, it is the safety and love of a good church, a church where people love one another and can express their suffering and fears, finding help and intercession.

But the one simple fact is this: you need a place where you can cry out in desperation and throw it all upon God as Jehoshaphat did when he cried, *"Oh God, don't You rule over all the kingdoms of the heathen? Don't You possess all power and might, so that none is able to withstand You? God, Your reputation is tied to us! We have no might against this army. We do not know what to do. But we are looking to You." And there, with wives and children, the people cried to the Lord affirming their dependency on God's mercy.* (Paraphrased from 2 Chronicles 20: 6-13)

GETHSEMANE IS MORE THAN A PLACE TO CRY

Gethsemane is not the garden of complaint or murmur. Oh no! Gethsemane is much more than that. Gethsemane is the place you discover the deepest mystery of the cross – your love for God. For there, in Gethsemane, is where men of honor rise, embrace the pain, the rejection, the horror and say to the Lord, "not my will but Thine be done." (Luke 22:42 KJV)

Your life will change in Gethsemane. There, in that place before God, you will see the horror as God does. You will see the injustice and understand – the ungodly shall not prosper! There, in Gethsemane, you will understand that you were not a victim – you were chosen.

God is in Gethsemane. It is there that He meets you in your need. It is there that He gives you the revelation of what He sees, and you realize it is not a tragedy after all – it is a triumph!

From Gethsemane, you will fasten your grip upon the hand of God; His will becomes your will. You will receive humiliation as glory. You will take the reproach and wear it as a crown. You will drink the cup. You will embrace the shame, the pain.

There, in Gethsemane, you say yes to God. And when you do, you say yes to the cup of affliction, which may include your family forsaking you and the cruel taunts of the crowds. Like Jesus, you say yes to the pain from the nails and the beating from the soldiers. Your yes in Gethsemane means you are willing to take on shame and humiliation as the world rallies fiercely against you and nails you to the cross. It means you will trust God as others portray you as evil, inflicting pain, and you begin to understand some will never trust you again and will, in fact, spend the rest of their lives trying to destroy yours. Saying yes in Gethsamane is giving your reputation fully to God, trusting His resurrection power, even as people spit on you, despise you, and are embarrassed of you. When you say yes in Gethsemane, you say yes to God!

LET US RISE AND BE GOING

You will leave Gethsemane. You cannot live there. Just like the cross, it is a passage, not a destination. Glory is the destination! Furthermore, you will leave Gethsemane differently than the way you arrived.

Jesus left Gethsemane by saying to His disciples, *Rise, let us be going.* (Matthew 26:46 KJV) He would not go alone. He was determined for them to be fully awake and present for the events soon unfolding. They watched Him in Gethsemane. They watched Him in His agony, and Jesus was determined they would watch Him in His glory, too.

It is as if Jesus is saying to His disciples, "Come with Me. You failed Me. You didn't pray for Me. You didn't comfort Me. But now, come with Me and behold My glory, My triumph." He was not rebuking them. Though He had every right to forsake them, He did not. He chose them to come and watch, to be with Him.

I appeal to many of you who are fed up with the church. The church slept while you were suffering. The church didn't pray for you. The church didn't comfort you. Please, don't throw the church away. Go to the church. Invite them to be with you. Tell them to rise and come with you. Let them be a part of the glorious things God will do through your life. Release the believers who failed you. Help them get out of Gethsemane with you. Encourage them like Jesus did the disciples; tell the church – you have seen me in my suffering, come with me and see me in my glory.

PUBLIC DECLARATIONS BECAUSE OF GETHSEMANE

Jesus was not sweating blood before Pilate. Jesus was not in agony before the Sanhedrin. Jesus was not pleading with God for a different way as He subjected Himself to false accusations before the High Priest. Instead, He was a soldier. He was unflinching. He was not the one on trial – hell was on trial, sin was on trial. He was not facing His judges; He was the judge.

Jesus would not leave Gethsemane weak, whimpering, and confused. Instead, He had His orders, and He was ready to go. He would be kind to the unkind. He would love the unloving. He would do the work while every voice blasphemed. He would sacrifice His life for the abusers. He would march like a soldier into victory. He would demonstrate to every living thing how much He loves and adores His Father.

What about you? How are you leaving Gethsemane? Are you different? Are you a man of honor? Will you be kind to the unkind? Will you fervently love the cold hard-hearted spouse you are married to? Will you do the work of God with joy? Will you pray and bless those who abuse you? Will you soldier on in the midst of pain and mockery? Will you demonstrate to every living thing how much you love and adore Jesus? When you think there is no hope, will you hope? When you cannot take it anymore, will you receive the Father's mercy, so you do not faint?

In the private Garden of Gethsemane, we cry, suffer, and plead. However, in public, we are soldiers with the shout of victory – because we cried in Gethsemane. In the private Garden of Gethsemane, we cry to our God. However, in public, we decorate His sacred honor with our praise!

Yes, cry, pour it out to God. But get up from there with the conviction that the Lord is your God and rejoice. For those who kneel before God in Gethsemane will sit as kings before their enemies!

Jesus' demeanor carrying the cross was totally different than His demeanor while laying over a rock and sweating blood in Gethsemane. There goes Jesus marching out of Gethsemane, making His Father look glorious. He was the Lamb King marching to vanquish hell and sin. I imagine Jesus thinking, as He carried that cross to Calvary: you see Me carrying a cross, but I see Me carrying an atomic bomb. You see Me walking in the will of the Romans, but I see Me walking in the will of my Father. You see Me walking in defeat, but I see Me walking in victory. You see Me as the spectacle of men, but I see Me as the darling of heaven, the adoration of angels. I am not a prisoner of Rome – I am the warden of the prison of Hope!

HOW DO YOU REPRESENT GOD?

Life here, in this corrupt world, is not about our particular happiness. Life, all of life, is about communion with God and making Him look glorious. Regardless of what you say you believe, the truth of your testimony is all about how you represent God. This is what makes a man of honor.

The beauty of Jesus' love for His Father was demonstrated by His glorious suffering. Sure, Jesus could have called for a legion of angels. Imagine the stateliness of that possible scenario. Heaven opens, a legion of angels descends, the masses of humanity humiliated as they realize the bond between Jesus and the Father in heaven. But instead, Jesus dried His tears and joyfully took the cross to perform what would most please His Father. It was not in the demonstration of power that Jesus proved His love for His Father; rather, it was in the posture of suffering! Likewise, you also have the opportunity to prove your love for God by your posture of suffering. Sure, God could annihilate or incapacitate Satan on your behalf. Obviously, people would be impressed with your relationship with God. However, the lasting impression of your love for God will not be in the moments of power but in the moments of suffering joyfully!

The beauty of the Father is seen through you when you renounce the promises of Satan and take pleasure in the greater glory of Christ. Take Job as an example. There he is, on his ashes. No doubt he is devastated in pain and suffering. Instead of rejoicing in God because the storm did not take the lives of his children or that angels came down from heaven and destroyed those who robbed his wealth, he sits bankrupt before the world and cries, *Though He slay me, yet will I trust in Him.*

(Job 13:15 KJV) Suffering joyfully for God's glory shows the world how deeply your heart adores and worships the Lord.

You can't fake joy in the midst of suffering. You can try, but people can smell the hypocrisy a mile away. Taking the cup of pain in Gethsemane and joyfully marching to the cross is supernatural.

Mine is a valid joy because I'm happy in Jesus even if I must drink the cup. If I am called to carry sickness or be despised, then I will bear it joyfully for the One my soul adores. I will not spend my time whining about life – I will rejoice. I will not live blaming people. I will forgive them. I will not live with bitterness because of my wounds; instead, I will be healed and help others heal. I will not blame the church, people, or circumstances; instead, I will take every occasion to be like Christ. I will not go around thinking that I have all the problems; instead, I will consider myself chosen - chosen to be an expression of love to the world for my beautiful Father.

SOLDIER ON

Do not take Gethsemane with you to the cross. Leave it there: the confusion, the agony, and the trouble. Rise up, soldier. March on, man of honor. Embrace the place that God has called you to. The mockers do not win! Pilate does not win. The Romans do not win. You are chosen to bear the glory of the Father. Everything—the persecution, the famine, the peril, the sword—does not change the fact that you are more than a conqueror through Him that loves you. You win! God wins! And triumph will be displayed throughout eternity.

Be different than the others. Because you had a Gethsemane, you shall have a resurrection. Be careful how you act, how you speak. The soldier marching into war does not speak of death but life: the life of heaven, the life of Jesus, the life of victory, the life of forgiveness, the life of freedom, the life of joy. Don't walk with your head down. Don't live depressed. Don't give the impression that you are a victim of bondage. Nobody forced you to follow Christ! No, sir, you volunteered!

DO NOT BYPASS GETHSEMANE

You cannot skip Gethsemane for Calvary. You cannot bear the cross without the garden. You will not endure the suffering. You need the place of crushing first. You need to cry. You need to pour out your lamentation and fears.

Refuse Gethsemane, and you will be destroyed. You may miss the resurrection from all this suffering. If you refuse your Gethsemane, you will come to believe that your crucifixion was something unjust and meted out by cruel men. Your life will end up defined as a victim. You will blame God. You will blame the church. You will blame people. You will live oozing out the infections of abuse and injustice. Your life will forever look like abuse. Your life will scream, "I was abused. I was mistreated. You do not know what they did to me. They ruined my life. I will never trust people again."

Perhaps that is where some of you are. You shrink back and think, "Oh God, that is me. I'm bitter and angry. I missed the glory. I missed my Gethsemane." I have good news for you! If you have already been crucified and missed your Gethsemane, it is not too late. Like you, most people miss their Gethsemane. As I minister to people about

Gethsemane, numbers have considered the fact – I did not know there was a place I could cry and protest. I did not know there was a place where God would comfort me to move forward. Could this be the reason that I am so unlovable, so untrusting, so angry?

Here is your good news. You can still have your Gethsemane. God is redemptive; He is able to recover you from all the damage that has afflicted you. Jonah had his Gethsemane in the belly of the whale. Gethsemane is the place where you agree with God, where God's will becomes your will.

As the Father comforts you in His love and as you affirm to Him your devotion, you are now the victor. You are not at the mercy of your enemies; you are chosen! That is the marvel of Gethsemane. Mary and Martha had their Gethsemane after Lazarus died. They cried to the Lord, "Where were you? You could have healed him." Maybe your Gethsemane will happen the moment you close this chapter!

Oh, and how do you know when you have had your Gethsemane? Good question. Simple answer. You know you have had your Gethsemane when you can say, "Father, forgive them, for they know not what they do."

FAITH TO OVERCOME POSING

Have you ever pretended to be something or someone you are not? Have you acted, said, and done things out of character because of who is around you, portraying yourself differently in groups than you would one-on-one? Perhaps you have behaved inauthentically because you were embarrassed about being yourself, or maybe you tried to fit in with people because you wanted them to notice or like you. Acting out a lie or deceiving someone just to be accepted are all characteristics of being a "Poser."

People can pose so well and maintain this behavior for so long that they do not even realize they are doing it, losing sight of who they are. Then, when they are alone, they worry they cannot keep up the lie, and the pressure builds. There is a burden to maintaining the façade of being someone we are not. We can lose ourselves by playing a role of a person who does not exist. This can lead to betraying family or friends and hurting other people and organizations. Some posers have lost jobs, while others have caused divorces. Posers can lose relationships, cause church splits, harm businesses, and destroy ministries. When people pose too long, they eventually get caught, and the collateral damage can be extreme.

This world is full of posers. When you hear the word poser, do you think of anyone in particular? Let us look at some poser examples. The movie *Groundhog Day* had a main character who was a poser. And in the movies *Bruce Almighty* and *The Grinch,* there were extreme posers. There are more. How about the leading character in *Top Gun* or *Maverick?* These characters all illustrate someone trying to be something they are not.

Jesus talked about posers in the Bible. He said, *"Hypocrites! For you are like whitewashed tombs which indeed appear beautiful outwardly, but inside are full of dead men's bones and all uncleanness."* (Matthew 23:27 NKJV)

Jesus also talked about those who pray for show. He called posers hypocrites. *"And when you pray, you shall not be like the hypocrites. For they love to pray standing in the temple and on the corner of the streets, that they may be seen by men."* (Matthew 6:5 NKJV)

He told another group acting like posers, *"All right, but let the one who has never sinned throw the first stone!"* (John 8:7 NLT)

Let us look at one of Jesus' closest followers, Peter. Do you think he could be called a poser? Jesus said, *"Get behind Me, Satan; for your mind is not set on God's will or His values and purposes, but on what pleases man."* (Mark 8:33 AMP)

Today's platform of social media shows many posers. People pose all day long. Many posers are presenting the destination life, not the journey life. They show off their houses, cars, places they've visited, and extravagant gifts, all to project something false. They even make different pages and groups for the different posing they do. Posing can also be seen in politicians; in fact, some of them are professional posers.

Posing is one of the most difficult character traits to change. So let's get real with ourselves and find an accountability mentor/partner you trust. Then together, help one another, if necessary, with this issue and give it all to Christ. Come clean, ask for forgiveness, and start every day by renewing your mind and declaring who God says you are. *But be transformed and progressively changed by the renewing of your mind [focusing on godly values and ethical attitudes].* (Romans 12:2 AMP)

When thoughts arise that cause you to say things that are not true or act out something false or fake so that others will accept you, TAKE THOSE THOUGHTS CAPTIVE! (2 Corinthians 10:5) Because the lies, deceit, and acting damage your life and relationships and are debilitating to your walk with the Lord. If this is you, give posing to Christ and repent, change your habits by asking God to strengthen you in this area, and start new by putting on the mind of Christ.

Put on your armor instead of putting on the facade. Realize it is a daily battle to take your mind and emotions captive. Yes, you can stop "posing." We do not battle against people, but we wage war against spiritual powers, the tempter, and the temptation of habits. (Ephesians 6:12-14) ARMOR UP, MEN. Every morning put your helmet of salvation (which covers your mind/emotions) along with the belt of truth to be set free. This is the only way to become who and what you are called to be—a man of honor, a man who overcomes adversity through faith.

. . . .

UNITED MEN OF HONOR:
OVERCOMING ADVERSITY THROUGH FAITH

SEAN M. HEALEY

Sean is a husband and a father to four beautiful boys. And he is a warrior for the Kingdom of God.

Sean served in the United States Army and is currently finishing a degree in Christian Counseling at Liberty University. Taking his passion for Jesus outside the church, Sean leads a street evangelism ministry in Lehigh Acres, Florida.

As a member of the Southwest Florida Band of Brothers, Sean is focused on the hearts of men, going to war with the enemy, and impacting the world with the Gospel of Jesus Christ.

FROM ABORTION TO ADOPTION

BY SEAN M. HEALEY

I spent my earliest years with my mom and my grandmother. As a small child, I spent Sundays sitting on my grandmother's lap watching football; other than that, it was just mom and me. We were always together. Whether going grocery shopping, to a doctor's appointment, to the park, or just on another random errand, it was always just the two of us. You see, my dad was nothing more than a one-night stand, and when he found out my mother was pregnant, he wanted her to get an abortion. From a very young age, I knew I was not wanted.

Life with my mother and my grandmother was good. Despite not having a dad around, I felt loved by the women in my life. My mom did not have much, and we moved a lot for the first few years of my life. I grew up without feeling a sense of home, except for the short period of time we lived at my grandmother's house. However, even though the life I had been born into was not glamorous or privileged, I was a happy child. I was not sure why my dad and my mom were not together, why she would not let me see him, or 1why he did not want me. Nonetheless, I was a happy kid. Life was not perfect, but it was nice. Little did I know that when I was five, everything would change.

Being a single mom, my mother would date regularly. In the first few short years of my life, I was introduced to a handful of my mom's flings. Some of my mom's flings were boyfriends, and some were just another one-night stand. I did not realize it then, but my relationship with men became extremely distorted at an early age. Not only did I not understand why my real dad was missing from the picture, but I was confused by the various men entering and exiting my life. When I was five, my mom finally gave up the dating scene and introduced me to the man who would become my stepfather. My mom's life of dating various men was finally over but unfortunately, so was the life of joy I had known before meeting my stepfather.

Right from the start, I knew things would be different. My stepfather John was an incredibly angry and abusive man. When John was young, his dad abused him and eventually left his mother for another woman. John's dad started a brand-new family and acted as if John and his brothers didn't even exist. My stepfather was a damaged soul and took all his hurt and pain out on us. Having grown up with just my mom and my grandmother, I was a very gentle and passive child. I was very timid and did not understand the world of men or how to "act like a man." And it did not take long before I became completely terrified of John.

One morning while I was home alone with John, I fell off my new bike, scraping it up. Looking for help and hoping for some comfort, I ran inside to tell John what had just happened. To my horror, it was not help or comfort that John responded with; instead, he threw me across the living room, and I was abused for the first time in my little life. I was in shock. I had never been spanked or even yelled at by my mother or grandmother. All I had known up to that point was love. It was at that very moment that I knew my life was never going to be the same. I knew that the world I had experienced before, one filled with joy and gentle guidance, was a world that would now be filled with a dark and abusive presence. I was scared, and I had no idea what to do. Thankfully, even though I had no idea at that time who God was or what Jesus did for me on the cross, He was already working things out for my good. Jeremiah 29:11 tells us, *"For I know the plans that I have for you," declares the Lord, "plans for prosperity and not for disaster, to give you a future and a hope."* (NASB) Even though I did not live in a Christian home or attend a church, and despite not even knowing the name Jesus, God was already working to save me from the hell I was about to live in for the next decade.

The next few years of my life were horrible. We lived in a rundown apartment; I changed schools frequently and was constantly in a state of fear. When I was seven, my little brother Nick was born. Though we had a big age difference, I quickly learned to love the little guy. I had always wanted a sibling and thought it was great having a little brother around. However, though I enjoyed my new little brother, it quickly became evident to me that I was now the outcast. John finally had a son of his own, and it was no secret that he loved Nick in a way I had never experienced. I began to grow cold, and I began to resent everybody around me. I was mad at John and hated him even to the point of wishing he were dead. I was mad at my little brother for no justifiably good reason other than he was loved and I was not. Lastly, I was angry with my mom for choosing John and allowing him to hurt me as he did. I was just a small child, but I was consumed by large amounts of hate, rage, and depression. I was lost.

When I was eight years old, my family decided to leave the only environment I had ever known and move to the backwoods of Vermont. Promises of dirt bikes, fishing, and adventure quickly faded and went unkept. Life in Vermont became miserable, and I was more isolated and afraid than I had ever been in my life. My brother and I grew farther apart, my relationship with my parents grew more turbulent, and I began to rebel against everyone and everything. School became a place for me to escape and stopped being a place to learn. My grades were bad, my behavior took a turn for the worse, and I even had to sit with a school psychologist. I was heading down a dark path, and no one seemed to care. Instead of conversations and loving guidance, my behavior was met with emotional and physical abuse. Instead of learning and growing from my mistakes as a child, I was pushed deeper into the dark and angry world that was already forming around me. Not only was I changing, but I began to grow colder and colder by the day.

By the time I reached middle school, I had discovered gangster rap, sex, and drugs. I submerged myself in a world where I could be as violent, cold, and brutal as I wanted to be. I cared about no one, and I listened to no one. After growing up for years hearing how stupid and how much of a failure I was, I developed a callused and hardened heart. The sweet, joyful, and gentle young man I used to be was gone. My parents moved us out of state again, and I started my freshman year of high school in Florida. By that time, I was a full-grown monster.

Insecure, scared, and immature, I quickly learned the art of posing. I made myself into something I was not, and I kept that act up for years. I started hanging out with the wrong friends and began using drugs frequently. I smoked weed every day, ate acid and shrooms, did ecstasy on the weekends, had sex, robbed people, and fought whenever the opportunity arose. I eventually ran away from home and lived on the streets. When my mom would find me, she would bring me home, only for me to run away again. I hated my life, I hated my family, I hated school, and all I wanted to do was escape reality.

Ephesians 1: 4-5 says, *Even as He chose us in Him before the foundation of the world, that we should be holy and blameless before Him. In love He predestined us for adoption as sons through Jesus Christ, according to the purpose of His will.* (ESV) God has always had a plan for my life; I just could not see it and did not know it. I was always destined to be a United Man of Honor; I just could not fathom it. It was not until I was nineteen years old that I finally met the God who not only loved me but was the only true Father I would ever have. My whole life, I lived as an orphan. Looking back now, it was a simple phone call that changed everything.

One morning as I was sitting on my couch in my room, I noticed an ad for the Army. I really just wanted the free stopwatch they were offering, so I called to request the giveaway. Shortly after, I found myself enlisted in the United States Army and heading off to basic training. After completing basic training, I had a weekend to relax with my new brothers. During that weekend, I met a girl, and we spent much of the weekend together. A few weeks later, I was heading to Korea and had a layover in Seattle. Knowing that the new girl I just met was from Portland, I thought I would try and close the deal with her. She offered to pick me up and let me stay at her aunt's house for the weekend. I gladly accepted and fully believed that by the end of the weekend, we would be having sex. Honestly, all I wanted was sex from this girl, and I was going to do whatever I could to get what I wanted.

While in Seattle, I played the good guy act. I acted as if I were a caring and nice guy, but in reality, I was just a player looking for sex. While staying at her aunt's house, her aunt began to tell me about a man named Jesus. She told me how she had been into witchcraft, and Jesus saved her from a literal hell. Interesting as it all was, my sights were only focused on accomplishing my mission. The next day I was invited to church by the girl's family, and I reluctantly said yes (after all, I was a good guy, right?). At the end of the church service, the pastor asked if there was anyone who was not right with God and if so, to raise their hand. Without hesitation, I raised my hand. To my surprise, the pastor then asked those who had raised their hands to come to the front for prayer. Knowing that everyone had seen me, I reluctantly went with the flow. I walked up to the front of the church, and a gentleman prayed for me. After the prayer, he asked me if I'd like to go somewhere quiet to talk. Screaming, "No way!" inside my head, I said, "Yes," and went with him.

When I walked into the room, I noticed a statue of Jesus and, surprisingly, though the church had thousands of people attending, no one else was in the room with us. The gentleman asked me if I had ever given my life to Jesus and if I wanted to. Even though I had no interest in what he said, I went along with everything and hoped I could escape the conversation as soon as possible. I did not care about God. I did not know Jesus. I had no sorrow for the things I had done, and I knew nothing about the Christian faith. I just wanted out of the room I was in so I could get a few more hours with the girl I was trying to make it with before my flight. However, God had different plans for me. Leading me to an altar and kneeling before the statue of Jesus, the gentleman began to pray in tongues. I had no idea what was going on, and to be honest, I was a little freaked out. The gentleman kept asking me to repeat after him, but I had no idea what he was saying or what to think. But, to put an end to the awkward situation I was in, I decided to try. It was at that very moment my life changed forever.

When I opened my mouth, everything went black. The only thing I remember is opening my eyes and something like electricity flowing through my entire body. I was terrified but also felt total peace. I was confused but also felt so sure about what I felt. I know now that it was the Holy Spirit who overcame me and entered me. Despite all the horrible things I had done in my life, God made Himself known to me. Truly, it was as the Bible says in Matthew 18:12, *What do you think? If any man has a hundred sheep, and one of them goes astray, will he not leave the ninety-nine on the mountains, and go and search for the one that is lost?* (NASB)

The gentleman looked at me and said, "It feels good, doesn't it?" I simply nodded my head yes, and then he took me to the gift shop. He bought me a Bible and a *Third Day* CD. Before we went our separate ways, the gentleman told me I would come under attack from my newly aroused enemy, who would tell me that what had happened was not real in an attempt to lead me astray. Unfortunately, that is exactly what happened. A few hours later, I got on a plane and flew to Korea.

With no idea what just happened, no mentorship, and no church to plug into, I spent the next decade believing in God but remaining very far away from Him. But just like in Genesis 3:9, *But the Lord God called to the man and said to him, "Where are you?"* (ESV), God never stopped pursuing me.

Years later, I met my wife, and we both decided to seek God. My wife came from an overly religious home where Jesus was used as a weapon against her. She emancipated her parents at sixteen and had been running from God until the very day we met. Together, we decided to seek Jesus, not knowing what the journey would bring. A few years later, we both made a decision to give our lives to Christ publicly and get baptized.

My wife and I currently have four beautiful little boys, a nice house, make great money, and we are both healthy and serving God! It has been a long road, and I have made too many mistakes to count. At times, I have failed as a father, a husband, and a friend. But God has been with me every step of the way, and I can proudly say that I am a new man, a United Man of Honor, a man transformed by the mercy and grace given to me by God. I was once just a scared and lonely child whose father wanted to abort him. Then I became a destructive and angry young man. But now, I am a loving husband, a caring father, and an adopted son of Jesus Christ. Thanks to God, I went from abortion to adoption. I am wanted and I am loved by the best Father ever. So are you.

JAN SCHER

Jan and his wife Melanie have been married for 41 years and reside in Sunrise, Florida. They have three daughters and three grandkids. Jan grew up in Queens, New York, and relocated to South Florida after graduating high school. He received an AA from Miami Dade Community College and his Bachelor of Science in Criminal Justice from Florida International University.

Jan worked for 18 years in law enforcement before retiring to run and operate his own financial servicing company with his wife, Melanie. Jan loves spending time with his family and friends, especially his grandkids. He enjoys traveling, sports, taking his dog for car rides, dad jokes, and acronyms.

Born and raised Jewish, Jan accepted Jesus Christ as his Lord and Savior at age 45. He loves spending time in God's Word and is honored to serve on the leadership team of the Florida Band of Brothers Bootcamp Ministry. He is a Forgiving Forward Coach and believes we need to be bold in our faith and in the mighty power of Prayer and Forgiveness through God's GRACE – God's Riches At Christ's Expense.

FINDING YOUR PLACE IN THE STORY

BY JAN SCHER

Do you ever feel there's more to life and you are not where you want to be financially, spiritually, or in your career or relationships? And you can't get out of your own way? It's like you are living on a treadmill or starring in the movie *Groundhog Day*.

I knew that was the case for me at age 59 years old. I wanted to do better and be better, but I couldn't get out of my own way. No matter how much I wanted to change, I kept self-destructing and living a life of existence.

My hope, prayer, and desire is that sharing the personal story of my journey of finding faith through adversity will help someone else find their peace of heart and their place and purpose in the story.

My name is Jan Scher. I'm 69 years of age and have been married to my beautiful wife Melanie for over 40 years. We have three daughters,

Samantha, Melissa, and Heather, and three grandkids, Camden, Riley, and Wyatt.

I was born in New York City, which you would probably recognize if you could hear my accent. I have an older sister and brother. We were raised by our parents in a lower-middle-income, liberal Jewish home. I was bar mitzvahed at age 13; however, if I were any less religious, I would be considered a borderline atheist.

I was never physically or sexually abused, homeless, hungry, or had an alcohol, drug, gambling, or pornography addiction. But I did have a father who was physically present but emotionally checked out and a mother who loved us conditionally.

My dad was void of any outward affection or encouragement and never told my siblings or me he loved us. I don't know what is worse, having a dad you never know or one who is physically present in your life but emotionally invisible and checked out.

I found out in my early 20s that my dad's father hadn't died, as I had been told, but actually went out to buy a pack of cigarettes one night when my dad was five years old and never came back. He abandoned the family.

My parents divorced during my senior year of high school after 26 years of marriage. Both my parents subsequently remarried and have since passed away. I have hardly spoken to and have not seen my sister and brother since my mom's funeral in 2014 due to wounds and circumstances I caused while my mom was still with us.

I know my parents loved us and did the best they could to raise us, but hurt people hurt people, intentionally or unintentionally, because you can't fix what you don't know is broken.

I remember crying when my mom told my brother and me she and my father were filing for divorce. However, the next day, after getting over the initial shock, I realized it was for the best and thought, *How did they stay together for as long as they did the way they treated each other?*

I made an agreement/promise to myself that day that when I got married and had a family of my own, I would never ever act, behave, or treat my wife and kids the way my parents did us and each other. However, what I discovered is the more you focus on not doing or behaving a certain way, the closer it draws you in to becoming that person you were trying to avoid. I found out that what you focus on, good or bad, is what you become or how you act.

I became my parents. I was conditionally loving towards my wife and kids and checked out, becoming emotionally isolated. I was all surface and no substance in every area of my life and lived a life of existence.

You can only do what you know or observe, and I subconsciously withdrew emotionally. I escaped and isolated myself by watching television and movies. I had a 3-6 hour-a-day addiction/habit. I found out that sin grows best in the dark.

As a result of my behavior, or lack of it, I had some success in my personal and business life but never reached my God-given potential as a husband, father, grandfather, or businessman. I knew God had more in store for me, but I couldn't make the changes I needed. Asking for help was not an option because, to me, that was a sign of weakness. And it was definitely out of my emotional comfort zone.

> *"For I know the plans I have for you," declares the Lord, "plans to prosper you and not harm you, plans to give you hope and a future." (Jeremiah 29:11 NIV)*

I would use my sense of humor as the first line of defense to keep people at an emotional distance. For example, "Did you hear about the banker who got rid of his girlfriend? He lost interest!!!" Well, so did I.

As I was wandering in the desert for the first 58 years of my life, searching for direction and change, God placed people in my life to help me. But I was too spiritually unaware to realize it at the time.

> *Rejoice always, pray continually, give thanks in all circumstances; for this is God's will for you in Christ Jesus. (1 Thessalonians 5:16-18 NIV)*

My wife Melanie, who was raised Catholic and has always been strong spiritually, never pressured me religiously and gave me the freedom to find my way to God on my timetable and terms. In the fall of 1995, I started to attend a Bible study at my office hosted by a fellow business associate. I went in an attempt to get answers and to figure out why I was stuck in a rut and couldn't get out of my own way. I was given a Bible to read by my friend K, the host of the study, and I learned at the age of 42 that Jesus was a Rabbi. Who knew? In subsequent discussions, Ms. K advised that it's not about religion but about having a personal relationship with God. Once you establish that relationship, it's like God is talking directly to you as you read His word in the BIBLE = Basic Instructions Before Leaving Earth.

After going through an intensive internal conflict between my Jewish faith of birth and my spiritual draw to Christianity, I accepted Jesus Christ as my Lord and Savior on 01/27/1999. I was disappointed after making that difficult decision, however, for nothing significantly changed in my life – there was no music playing or angels flying, and I was still the same. I subsequently made two or three additional altar calls over the next several years, reconfirming my acceptance of Jesus Christ as my Lord and Savior. But still, there were no major changes in my life.

In the fall of 2012, I was involved in a very stressful arbitration hearing through my business, which created emotional, financial, and medical challenges due to the consuming amount of time, energy, and stress involved. I had retired from the police department after 18 years of service to start our family business with my wife and had testified hundreds of times as an officer. But I had never experienced anything like that hearing. It was the most stressful event in my life.

A friend of mine named Mike was going through a similar situation, which we discussed at a company function. Mike's 4-year-old granddaughter told him to stop worrying about "those bad men" and pray and forgive them for their actions. Wisdom out of the mouth of babes. So, during the hearing, I took Mike's grandkid's advice and prayed every day for all those people who had accused me of wrongdoing. And then I asked that God would forgive them for what they had done.

Additionally, at a lunch break during the proceedings, Mike asked me to pray over our food in front of all the attorneys and home office staff. I was not comfortable in prayer and had never prayed aloud, especially in public, and I was not a happy camper. This just added to my already shot nerves. But, I reluctantly agreed out of respect for Mike's confidence in me and the sheer embarrassment I would experience if I didn't pray. Honestly, I can't remember anything I said, but I was totally upset and disappointed when I finished, thinking I sounded like a babbling fool. I later learned, however, that there's no right or wrong way to pray if the prayer is from your heart and that we need to be bold when sharing our faith.

> *Give praise to the Lord, proclaim His name: make known among the nations what He has done.* (Psalm 105:1 NIV)

If anyone is curious, after two weeks of presenting evidence and testimony, the Arbitration Panel dismissed all counts and claims against me and the company. The power of prayer and forgiveness.

In 2013, a friend and a business mentor named Guy invited me to my first - and the inaugural - Florida Band of Brothers Bootcamp. I attended reluctantly, not knowing what to expect based on Guy's creditability. The camp is based on the book *Wild At Heart* by John Eldredge. It was transformational. It changed my life as God began to work on my heart and soul during the quiet meditation sessions. Of course, the change did not occur overnight, but seeds were planted that weekend, and the harvest was coming.

In between the structured topics, such as The Wound, Posing, Spiritual Warfare, The Heart of a Man and a Woman, The Larger Story, and The New Name, there were 15-30 minutes of quiet reflection time. In those moments of designed silence, God would meet you and minister to whatever your needs were at that time in your life.

I was 58 years old when I attended my first Bootcamp and had never sat still for 20-30 minutes at a time in my life to reflect on anything, let alone to have God work on my spiritual needs, and I believe I'm not the exception but the norm.

> *The Lord will fight for you; You need only be still.*
> (Exodus 14:14 NIV)

During prayer time, a leadership team member named Jim walked me through a PROcess as he asked me to think about the first memory of my childhood that popped into my mind. It was strange, but the first thought I had was when I was either 4 or 5 years old, which I had totally forgotten. When my dad came home from work one day, I asked him if he would play catch with me. But he said he was too tired and went into the house and proceeded to watch TV for the remainder of the night. Does that sound familiar?

I didn't realize how something so incidental and long forgotten or suppressed could have such a negative impact, creating the wound it did. The message to my 4 or 5-year-old self was, *You're not worth my time. I'd rather watch TV by myself than spend any time with you.* Ouch.

Hurt people hurt people. Not intentionally, but you can't change or fix what you don't know is broken. I would wager that my dad's father did something similar to him. After all, he abandoned my dad and his family when my dad was only 5. I now know why I cry every time I watch Kevin Costner at the end of the movie *Field of Dreams* playing catch with his dad.

As a result of that experience at my first Bootcamp, I volunteered for the Leadership Team the next year and have served on the team ever since.

A week before my first Bootcamp as a Leadership Team Member, my mom passed away. She had lost her battle with throat cancer at the age of 91, one month shy of her next birthday. At my first leadership meeting, the team prayed for me over the loss of my mom. That was the first time in my life that anyone had ever prayed over me. I could feel the presence of the Holy Spirit as the group lifted my family and me in prayer.

Then, in 2015, Dr. Bruce Hebel, the author of the book *Forgiving Forward*, attended the Bootcamp as a special guest speaker. He addressed the leadership team about his book with a powerful message of forgiveness. After hearing him speak, I asked if he could meet with me during the camp to talk. He must have sensed my torment as he agreed to meet. We spent two hours talking about God and His grace, and he walked me through the *Forgiving Forward* protocols, led by the Holy Spirit.

This encounter had a profound impact on my heart and soul. I was able to forgive all the people who had hurt and wounded me, ask for forgiveness from those I had hurt or wounded, and then forgive myself - which was the hardest thing to do. As a result, I felt a huge weight lifted off of my shoulders. My heart and spirit felt lighter, and I wanted to share that feeling with my family and friends.

I learned at the camp that we live on a battleship, not a cruise ship, and the battle is between God and Satan for and over our hearts.

> *For our struggle is not against flesh and blood, but against the rulers, against the authorities, against the powers of the dark world and against the spiritual forces of evil in the heavenly realms.* (Ephesians 6:12 NIV)

> *Above all else guard your heart, for everything you do flows from it.* (Proverbs 4:23 NIV)

> *You will seek me and fine me when you seek me with all your heart.* (Jeremiah 29:13 NIV)

> *Jesus replied: "Love the Lord your God with all your heart and with all your soul and with all your mind."* (Matthew 22:37 NIV)

In the book *Forgiving Forward*,[1] there is a quote on page 28 that reads, "Bitterness is the poison we drink hoping someone else dies. Bitterness is to the heart wound what infection is to the skin wound." I believe that we confess to God for the forgiveness of sins, but we need to confess to each other for healing because wounds need fresh air to heal.

---

1   Hebel, Bruce Wayne and Toni Lynn. *Forgiving Forward: Unleashing the Forgiveness Revolution.* Bruce and Toni Hebel, 2011

> *Therefore, confess your sins to each other and pray for each other, so you may be healed. The prayer of a righteous person is powerful and effective.* (James 5:16 NIV)

On page 43 in *Forgiving Forward,* Dr. Bruce and Toni Hebel write, "He (God) withholds His protection from us when we refuse to forgive. Why? Because unforgiveness is a sign we have devalued God's forgiveness of us, and it reveals our hearts are not grateful. In essence, our refusal to forgive others dishonors the price Jesus paid for our salvation. As a consequence, God withholds the liberating affect *[sic]* of His salvation in our daily lives. This consequence works out in a particularly strange way when the person we choose not to forgive is ourselves."

> *For if you forgive other people when they sin against you, your heavenly Father will also forgive you. But if you do not forgive others their sins, your Father will not forgive your sins.* (Matthew 6:14-15 NIV)

Due to the significant emotional and spiritual impact of the *Forgiving Forward* message on my life, I began sharing the book and my story with others. However, as pivotal as meeting Dr. Hebel was in my spiritual walk, and it was, it didn't become transformational until I finally surrendered my heart to God two years later in 2017. I finally asked God for help and surrendered to Him when my life was imploding around me financially and spiritually, with challenges in both my marriage and business. That's when I called a friend and confessed my sins and fears so the healing could begin.

At that point, I discovered that God was waiting for me to fully surrender to Him with a broken spirit and a contrite heart. Like King David, I just needed to lose my pride and EGO – Easing God Out.

> My sacrifice, O God, is a broken spirit; a broken and contrite heart you, God, will not despise. (Psalm 51:17 NIV)

Our healing begins when we surrender to God, confess our sins, and ask for forgiveness. And when that happens, God wants us to use our personal stories of overcoming adversity through faith to help free others so they can do the same.

> But he said to me, "My grace is sufficient for you, for my power is made perfect in weakness." Therefore I will boast all the more gladly about my weaknesses, so that Christ's power may rest on me. That is why, for Christ's sake, I delight in weaknesses, in insults, in hardships, in persecutions, in difficulties. For when I am weak then I am strong. (2 Corinthians 12:9-10 NIV)

We all have a destiny designed by God – it's something you have most likely felt within you your whole life. Walking in that destiny begins with giving your heart to God and trusting Him with your feelings.

Don't settle for less than God has created you for, but find your place through faith, forgiveness, and a settled and surrendered heart. And then go, share your story of victory with others and lead a life of SIGNIFICANCE instead of one of existence.

> *Each of you should use whatever gift you have received to serve others, as faithful stewards of God's grace in its various forms. (1 Peter 4;10 NIV)*

FAITH TO OVERCOME CONTROL

The Bible teaches us that God's sovereignty is an essential aspect of who He is—that He has supreme authority and absolute power over all things. Yet, many of us struggle in our lives trying to take over God's absolute power. We battle in our flesh, and we strive for the desire to control. It is part of the curse of sin that is ongoing.

We can believe being in control will make our lives better, but it is only a lie from Hell. We want to decide ourselves what is best for our lives and take over with force. But one day, we wake up to what God says and realize that life does not revolve around us, our thoughts, and our desires—as we once believed.

Think about the enemy of our souls and how he desires to capture our hearts. He tells us that control will give peace, safety, power, comfort, respect and so much more. But the more we feel out of control, the more we try to control—and it becomes a vicious cycle. The enemy will use this against us. Since when do we validate the enemy and give in to him by believing we know it all? We do not know what is best for us. Only God, in His infinite wisdom, sovereignty, and love, deems what is best for us. Proverbs 3:5-6 (TPT) describes this very well: *Trust in the Lord completely, and do not rely on your own opinions. With all your heart rely on him to guide you, and he will lead you in every decision you make. Become intimate with him in whatever you do, and he will lead you wherever you go.*

Dying to ourselves and our desire to maintain control is not easy. It takes humility and courage to admit, both to God and ourselves, that we have a problem we can't handle. It's essential to take time with God and recognize that He is in control; we are not God, we are not all-knowing, and we do not reign over the universe. Trusting God for your circumstances, relationships, and choices requires extreme focus and discipline. However, overcoming your own will and surrendering to His will can help you become confident—confident in knowing that His plan is the best plan. Keeping yourself in submission to God will make lasting differences in your life.

> But I discipline my body and keep it under control, lest after preaching to others I myself should be disqualified. (1 Corinthians 9:27 ESV)

Submitting our control to God brings Him glory and gives Him the ability to fulfill His purpose in us. However, when we think we have the best plan and try to control other people or the outcome of situations, God will always confirm that we do not have control; He does.

> For I know that nothing good dwells in me, that is, in my flesh. For I have the desire to do what is right, but not the ability to carry it out. (Romans 7:18 ESV)

As you surrender control to God, remember to pray and seek Him first before making any decision, and be comforted knowing what He says in Isaiah 55:8-9 NIV: *"For my thoughts are not your thoughts, neither are your ways my ways," declares the Lord. "As the heavens are higher than the earth, so are my ways higher than your ways and my thoughts than your thoughts."*

Go before the Lord and talk to Him. Spend time doing this as you pray about relinquishing all control to God. Read His Word and understand that the more you know about Him, the more you learn His character. Listen to Him when He speaks and thank Him because He is so very good. Be assured that God knows what He is doing in your life, and watch as the big things you seek to control become little in His hands. God promises to cover everything you need.

. . . .

LAURENT MINGUEZ

 Laurent Minguez is the president of Heavenly Hands and chairman of the board for Heavenly Hands Foundation. He is a husband and a father of five children. Laurent's faith has led him into marketplace ministry, where he mentors people by identifying skills and talents and investing in them through business ventures. His unique approach to doing business has enabled him to build a community of like-minded entrepreneurs to place God as the owner of their companies on paper. He has taken the concept of God, family, and business and created an all-in-one principle that God connects the family by doing business together.

Laurent is on the adventure of a lifetime with conflict resolution and risk-taking. Every step has been about seeking the will of God first while denying the flesh. God has been working through him to save souls, reveal the talents and calling in people's lives, and build community and faith in the marketplace. His priority is opening the mind, body, and spirit of his brothers and sisters. If you'd like to get in touch with him for a vision-meeting, he can be reached by email: Laurent@HeavenlyPros.com or cell phone: (561) 403-8542

GOD OWNS THE EARTH AND EVERYTHING IN IT

BY LAURENT MINGUEZ

The small business owner is the backbone of America. I don't believe we can say the same for any other nation on Earth.

What it takes to be a small business owner goes beyond school. It requires grit, work ethic, vision, organization, and people skills. A business owner doesn't clock in or out and can constantly be at risk of failure. I find it amazing that our country is carried by so many successful entrepreneurs.

My story begins with this calling of becoming a business owner, just like my father. My father built an empire, and I wanted to do the same. My initial desires as a child were to be able to offer my friends and family well-paying jobs in a fun and exciting environment. Little did I know that this child's dream would eventually become an addiction to power and money. How many of us can say we are addicted to money? And how many people have strayed away from our calling because of that desire?

The Word of God says, *Those who desire to be rich fall into temptation and a snare, and into many foolish and harmful lusts which drown men in destruction and perdition. For the love of money is a root of all kinds of evil, for which some have strayed from the faith in their greediness, and pierced themselves with many sorrows.* (1 Timothy 6: 9-10 NKJV)

I believe this to be a curse from the enemy. Worldly items are a great source of distractions.

I was one of the many who fell victim to the "rat race." I wanted to make money so much that I completely forgot about my dream. I was consumed, and without even realizing it, the desire for riches pulled me away from my true calling. My way of life during those days was all about the power of attraction. I only cared about what the world could do for me and how I could receive it. My selfish desires were manifesting. I made money and had a thriving career, a wife, children, and a beautiful home by the time I was in my early twenties. Life should've been good, and it was good, but only on paper.

Although I had just about everything my heart desired and was a "good person" in my own eyes, there was this big gaping hole in my heart. I started feeling sadness, discomfort, and emptiness. Little did I know, God was pulling on my heartstring and calling my name.

I've heard many testimonies of people hitting rock bottom before coming to the Lord, but my experience was nothing like that. Surprisingly enough, I was playing tennis one day when the man who was playing on the court next to me walked up and asked if I was interested in playing tennis with him. As our conversation progressed, he asked if I was a Christian. I responded by telling him that I believe in everything. If you think it, believe it, then it becomes reality. He laughed and asked if I'd read the Bible before. My answer was that I hadn't, but it was on my list of things to do. Let's just say that after that conversation, reading the Bible suddenly made its way to the top of the list. This gentleman ended up inviting me to his home the next day, and I began my very first Bible study.

As soon as I opened the incredible story of our Maker and His people, I couldn't put it down. The rich history, the poetic writing, and the incredible stories captured my complete and undivided attention. At that moment, I made a commitment to read the Bible from cover to cover without delay. Little did I know that through my reading method, I would learn about Judaism even before learning about Jesus.

During my time reading the Bible, I began to notice a shift in the way I acted and how I saw the world. I became a man of "The Law." Eat clean, work hard, wake up early, hit the gym, honor the sabbath, discipline your children, be the head of your home, keep track of every penny, tithe, and remain focused at all times.

This new way of life was exhausting and impossible to maintain, no matter how hard I tried. I felt I was not good enough or strong enough for God. Until one day, I finally made it to the New Testament and learned who Jesus was, and my world was shaken again. I realized that I didn't need to be perfect. All He wants from me is to have a deep and profound relationship with Him. He wants me to come as I am and simply love Him with all my heart, all my mind, and all my soul, and to love my neighbor as I love myself, as it states in Matthew 22:37-39. *'You shall love the Lord your God with all your heart, with all your soul, and with all your mind.' This is the first and great commandment. And the second is like it: 'You shall love your neighbor as yourself.'* (NKJV)

I didn't love myself when I was living in the law; I felt oppressed and lost my personality. But the shackles were broken at last, and the result was unbelievable: I became more like myself. I felt laid back and goofy; I started eating bacon and less healthy food again and slowed down going to the gym. In short, I renewed myself in Christ and felt peace.

After a short time, I realized I started gaining weight again and being less healthy as I slowed down on my stern way of life. Although it was relieving, it was unhealthy, and it seemed that I had backtracked physically.

As I kept reading through the New Testament, I learned about the Holy Spirit, the fruits of the spirit, and the power the Lord instills in us. I began experiencing the supernatural presence of God. He gave me clarity and a new desire and rebuilt me into a warrior for Christ.

As I reflected on this time before, during, and after my transformation, it was incredible to recognize the changes. I started as a rigid, by-the-book, stern man of God, became relaxed and filled with love, peace, and joy, and then found a sacred balance of an all-encompassing version of myself who found a renewed joy and desire to be healthy, physically active, and work hard. This all stemmed from my passion for Christ rather than adherence to the law.

In just a few short years, my entire being completely shifted. Little did I know this was just a warm-up for what God was preparing to do. Once I showed God that I was ready for the next phase of my life, my world became much more complex. And I learned that the enemy doesn't like it when we do God's work. He wants to destroy whatever God builds. My circumstance was no different. I began experiencing increased judgment from friends and family, difficult situations and conversations, and adversity, all because of my faith.

Even though I had never experienced so many problems before in my life, I was completely at peace because I knew that God was with me, and my empty heart was finally filled. The God-sized hole was now overflowing with love, passion, and clarity.

As I grew closer to the Lord, I began receiving very clear instructions from Him regarding the intentions He had for my life. He commanded me to build a ministry in the business marketplace, reminding me of my childhood desire to offer employment to friends and family and inspire them through the marketplace.

I dove into this deep desire to build a ministry within my business. I was a commercial real estate broker and had found a unique and successful niche that was teachable to other real estate agents. So I decided to make my first hire, my brother-in-law. My plan was to train him in our unique commercial sales tactics while inspiring and filling him with the Word of God and the Holy Spirit.

The results were amazing. His transformation began. He was held accountable at every step and was making a living for his family.

Now that the system was created, I hired four more team members who also experienced similar results as my brother-in-law. It was so unique to spend 40 hours with God every week and time with team members on the same wavelength, all while getting paid.

The enemy hated what we were doing, and we experienced tremendous adversity during the initial phase of God's plan, including COVID and dealing with agents from other companies who didn't like our operations and clients who did not appreciate the name of the company.

The name was *Heavenly Hands Realty*, and the logo was the hand of God coming out of the clouds. We weren't very subtle in our approach. As a result, we had both raving fans and terrible critics.

One night, I had a dream that I was walking with God. As we walked together, I asked Him, "How can I be of service to you, Lord? I want to do Your will and build Your Kingdom here on Earth. How can I be of service?"

He replied in such a simple manner. He said, *"Heavenly Hands. Change the name."*

Surprised at His response, I said, "What? Does the name not glorify you??!!"

His reply was, "It's too much."

Even though His words were simple, I felt a burst of emotions describing what He was saying to me. So I asked Him, "What do I change the company name to?"

To my surprise, I received a clear answer. *"Chosen."*

Immediately after that, I woke up and couldn't believe what had just happened. God spoke to me in my dream. I was speechless!

After receiving this message from God in my dreams, I was obedient and changed the company's name to *Chosen Real Estate Advisors*.

No sooner did I change the name of the company than God began to open new doors in an industry that I would've never expected -

construction. Although I'd owned a construction business for my own personal fix-and-flip properties, I wasn't actively pursuing that industry.

There we were, in the middle of COVID. I had just changed the name of my real estate company, and my brother-in-law, who was my first hire, was struggling with selling real estate. So we decided to pray together for guidance. Immediately, the presence of God came over me, and I asked my brother-in-law if he had any experience in construction. To my surprise, he said he had been in construction during his late teenage years and would be very interested in hearing more about my idea. So I immediately offered him a transitional position to manage a fix-and-flip renovation we were about to commence. With this change of position, his talent shone, and when I noticed the alignment, I decided to focus my time on building our renovation business to make sure we could sustain his new role.

God gave me a clear vision for the next phase of our business. We were to recruit small handyman business owners, collaborate and share resources, and build a community - because the construction industry needs Jesus!

During this time of transition, I had an incredible desire to find a way to make God the owner of my company on paper. As a Christian business owner, I always believed that God ran the show and that I was just riding as a passenger, but this wasn't enough for me. I truly wanted to be held accountable by God on paper. But I didn't know how to do this or if was it even possible.

I began reaching out to accountants and attorneys for advice on how to make God the owner of my company on paper, but no one could seem to provide any good ideas or insight. On the contrary, they were confused and couldn't understand why I would do such a thing. I kept hitting dead ends for months, but I was not ready to give up.

One day as I was at my wit's end on the idea of how to put God as the owner of my company on paper, I began a google search and typed, "What is a company with no shareholders." The results came back and sent me down the rabbit hole.

I came up with the definition of a non-profit organization under the Florida Statutes: "'Corporation not for profit' means a corporation no part of the income or profit of which is distributable to its members, directors, or officers." Or in simpler terms, it's a company with no shareholders.

Generally speaking, non-profits are utilized to not pay taxes to the IRS; however, I didn't care about the taxes. After all, my goal wasn't to avoid paying taxes but to make God the owner on paper.

So my idea for a non-profit began to form but was still not quite clear. The non-profit shows that there are no shareholders, but how do I deal with the IRS for approval?

Then it hit me, a shell non-profit organization that owns the for-profit. I could still pay taxes, follow the law, and point to God by expressing in the by-laws of the non-profit that God owns any for-profit under the non-profit. I couldn't believe how easy the solution to my dilemma was.

Now that the fundamental idea was in place, I was left to figure out how to ensure that we honor God in what He wants for His company and make it as least corruptible as possible.

As I continued my research, I kept noticing the significance of the number twelve in scripture, such as the twelve tribes of Israel and the twelve apostles. So I decided to follow suit with twelve board of directors in our non-profit.

Once we appointed the twelve board members, we began working on the by-laws for the non-profit. We actually took a lot of our rules from the original United States Constitution.

Once everything was in place and we were all in agreement with the governance of the Foundation, God began to bless His company to a new level. We went from being a small home improvement company to sitting down with major organizations, negotiating large contracts, being involved with breakthrough projects that happen once in a millennium, and hiring in excess of fifty employees in less than one year. It all happened in the blink of an eye.

Of course, when we are obedient to God, the enemy does not like it, and the enemy began his attack on our company. It started with gossip amongst employees, troublesome situations with customers, and significant delays in payment from clients all at once. We nearly missed payroll a few times.

My greatest fear was being unable to pay our team on time, and the enemy knew it. But God was in control. I would go to bed in fear, wondering how we would make payroll, and by morning, a payment from a customer would hit the account just in time to make payroll. It was a constant reminder that God was blessing our progress regardless of what the enemy was trying to do.

Then, I remember hearing God tell me to get ready because He was going to test my commitment to Him by making me go all-in with my personal finances, including my emergency funds.

As God promised, I was faced with His warning. I had to put God first in my finances by allocating a majority of my emergency savings to make payroll. It was gut-wrenching and extremely uncomfortable, especially the moment my wife realized what I had done.

But what happened next was a greater breakthrough than I could have imagined - I was about to receive the support and commitment from my wife on this crazy endeavor. First, she asked me why I took our family emergency money for the business. I told her that it was an emergency, and if I didn't do it, I wouldn't have made payroll. She explained that this money was specifically for family emergencies, and I agreed with her, explaining that this was, in fact, a family emergency. In her confusion, she asked me to elaborate. I responded by saying that this business is our ministry, and we are responsible for our family within our ministry.

In that moment, she realized what I had said and decided to support my crazy idea. She only asked one more question after that - did I believe that if our team members were faced with the same situation, they would do the same for us? My answer was that this is our assignment from God, we cannot compare what others would do, and we must fulfill God's calling on our lives because He is with us.

After that significant and uncomfortable conversation, my wife and I were never more aligned. She got involved with our ministry business, and I would never have imagined that this financial test would have created an even greater bond between my wife and me.

There is no doubt that God has been building His Kingdom here on Earth and utilizing all of us to fulfill that purpose. Knowing what I know now, by seeking Him with all my heart, mind, and soul, He has opened doors that can never be closed and shown me things that are indescribable. The level of fulfillment that He has given me has been incredible. And now that I know the impact God can make on my life, my family's life, and those who are a part of this story, I realize that this is only the beginning of an incredible story that will continue to impact many lives to come. It is also a reminder that I must continue to overcome adversity through faith and be the man of honor, united with my brothers and sisters, that God has called me to be.

FAITH TO OVERCOME FEAR

To overcome fear, we must be aware of its traps and be available to face them down. The fear of man can be one of the most significant roadblocks in life and in serving the Lord. Fear has the power to paralyze you. It takes faith to overcome fear. We can go right to God's Word for what the Bible instructs us to do.

> Be watchful, stand firm in the faith, act like men, be strong. Let all that you do be done in love. (1 Corinthians 16:13-14 ESV)

The fear of man is a trap, a snare that can lure, trap, and overpower us. When we make people big and give in to their power, we make God small. Peer pressure, codependency, and other things lead us to succumb to men and threaten to immobilize us. *Fear of man will prove to be a snare, but whoever trusts in the Lord is kept safe.* (Proverbs 29:25 NIV)

The fear of man is when people control how we think, feel, and act and it comes up when we view people as bigger and more significant than God in our lives. How can we be obedient to God's Word if we are concerned with what other people think of us?

There are two types of fear mentioned in the Bible. The first type is beneficial and encouraged, but the second type of fear is a detriment and is to be overcome.

The first fear spoken of in the Bible is the fear (respect) of the Lord, which brings about blessings and benefits, and is also the beginning of wisdom.

> The fear of the Lord is the beginning of wisdom and knowledge of the Holy One is understanding. (Proverbs 9:10 NIV)

The other biblical fear, the "spirit of fear," can come upon us at any moment and is something we must overcome. We can place all other fear into this category, even the fear of man. We need to trust and love God completely to rise above this type of fear. God reminds us that as He cares for the birds of the air, so much more will He provide for His children.

God will give you all the power to do what you are not capable of doing yourself. You need to be obedient as you go through your day, despite your fears. You must go in faith—trust in God that He will get you through any situation, whether you feel afraid, stupid, timid, or whatever it is that holds you back. Take a step through the fear even when you do not feel like it, ask God to help you, and watch His miraculous movement as He gives you the power to get beyond your fear.

All His life, Jesus faced people. He came up against people who hated Him, disagreed with Him, and looked down on Him. Did that stop Jesus? No, He humbled Himself And walked through whatever resistance came against Him so he could fulfill God's will. He is our greatest example. *For God has not given us a spirit of fear and timidity, but of power, love and self-discipline.* (2 Timothy 1:7 NLT)

Is fear holding you back from what God has called you to do? God's Word tells us, as Men of Honor, to be strong and courageous. Why? There is a reason He wants His men mighty and bold. God tells us not to be afraid of being alone or being too weak—so that we can stand for Him. He tells us not to be afraid—so our voices will not be muffled but will be heard above the crowd. He also commands us not to be afraid of lacking physical necessities—so we will focus on His purpose for our lives while always trusting His provision. There are admonishments through God's Word covering the various aspects of fear we should avoid. Put succinctly, we should never be stifled from living out our "calling in Christ" because of fear.

Once we have learned to put our trust in God and bravely walk forward by faith into the unknown, we will no longer be afraid of the things that will come against us. God takes our hand when we take the first step of faith forward. You serve the God of heaven's armies. Be a man of strength and valor. Be brave and of good merit in your home, work, church, and community. Fear has no dominion over a Man of Honor. Serve others and teach them to be the worthy man of God who fears God in all they do but does not fear man.

> *Be strong and of good courage, do not fear nor be afraid of them; for the Lord your God, He is the One who goes with you. He will not leave you nor forsake you. (Deuteronomy 31:6 NKJV)*

Lord, even when your path takes me through the valley of deepest darkness, fear will never conquer me, for you already have! You remain close to me and lead me through it all the way. Your authority is my strength and my peace. The comfort of your love takes away my fear. I will never be lonely, for you are near. (Psalm 23:4 TPT)

MICHAEL C. LOOMIS

 Michael Colt Loomis is an honest-to-goodness Florida native who spent three years behind enemy lines...in Georgia.

He is a graduate of the University of Florida and earned a Master's degree from Emory University, Candler School of Theology. He has served as the pastor of churches from Jacksonville to Miami.

Mike is currently the Lead Pastor of the New Life in Christ Church in Punta Gorda, Florida, where he has served for the last 12 years.

He likes kayaking, swimming, and reading in his leisure time.

Mike has been married for over 45 years to the love of his life, Debbie. Together they have four grown children (all of whom are girls except for three of them), and 13 grandchildren (and number 14 on the way).

Above everything else, he loves Jesus and is committed to Jesus as his Lord.

LOOMIS, YOU HAVE A PROBLEM!

BY MICHAEL C. LOOMIS

She began to throw everything made of glass.

Dad had left to go pick up milk and was gone too long. I have no idea if he was gone ten minutes or 5 hours. But, in Mom's mind, he was gone too long. So, she erupted in anger.

Everything my mom could put her hands on, she threw. By the time the night was over - when the screaming had ceased, the arguing was finished, and the throwing was done - Mom had broken every single item in the house made of glass. Everything. Every window, every cup, every plate, every mirror, the television - everything.

She also destroyed every one of my sister's (I will call her Cissy) presents.

I found Cissy in my mom's closet, curled up behind a long gown of mom's, shaking and sobbing.

It was my sister's 8th birthday.

This happened in the days when no one in Florida had air conditioning. Every window in every house in the neighborhood was wide open. Everyone heard what was going on. But the next day, no one said anything. I felt completely alone. I was nine years old. And I was miserable.

Our family's life was marked by anger and chaos. The result for Cissy and me was debilitating and lingering fear, exhibited by our own anger and depression.

When I was in the 5th grade, I remember my parents attending a Parent-Teacher Conference at school. I sat at a desk near the back of the room with my nose in a book, overhearing my teacher tell my parents how sad I seemed. I remember thinking, "I can fix that." I decided from that point on to "put on a happy face" to hide from the world.

I hid the sadness well. Yet, though it showed less, the sadness was still there. And the anger constantly smoldered under the surface of my life. I was angry with the world.

The next year, I got into six fights in one day with another kid in my class. I stole things. And I was introduced to pornography.

One Saturday, my dad felt something wrong physically. We went to the emergency room, where it was determined that he had a heart attack, likely from smoking two packs of cigarettes a day, drinking excessively, and being 40-50 pounds overweight. He was also in a high-stress occupation — a Lieutenant with the St. Petersburg Fire Department. As a result, he was forced to retire for medical reasons.

But, the drinking got worse, making things even more difficult for the rest of us.

When I was in the 8th grade, one night I needed to study for a Latin exam. Because Mom and Dad left me in the car while they hung out in a bar, I was forced to sit in the car and study, holding my book so the streetlight would shine on the verbs I was trying to learn and the vocabulary I was trying to memorize.

That same year, my dad got drunk and threatened to kill himself. I wrestled a loaded revolver away from him. I was 13.

One night, a friend from school invited me to a pool party at his house. While I was there, my dad showed up. He was drunk. I was embarrassed and ashamed, so I stayed in the pool, far away from my dad, hiding in the shadows.

The drinking escalated. The chaos intensified. Dad was a happy drunk, rarely getting mad – except when he and Mom went at it. But Mom would explode in rage when she drank.

In the fall of 1969, as a new sophomore in high school, I went to a varsity football game on a very hot Friday night in September. I was dressed in the fashion of the day – blue jeans and a white t-shirt. As the night wore on, I kept noticing this awful smell. I had no idea what it was. I did notice that people kept moving farther and farther away from me. Finally, there was no one within about 20 feet of me.

Someone yelled, "Loomis, you have a problem!"

I rode home from that game that night embarrassed, ashamed, and very self-conscious, with my head hanging out the car window because of the terrible stench.

I found out later that my dad had gotten some used t-shirts from a neighbor. He bleached them to make sure they were clean and white, but he had forgotten to rinse them. The bleach, combined with my body heat and sweat on that hot and humid Friday night, created a horrible odor. When my dad realized what had happened, he laughed. I fumed.

In October of that same year, my mom finally kicked my dad out of the house. His drinking had become so bad that he would fall out of bed.

I went to bed that night, afraid. I cried out to God, "If you're up there, and you're real, save my dad, or he'll die!"

That prayer was far more an act of desperation than an act of faith. I had no idea if God was real, or powerful, or even cared. I was just desperate. And in that desperate faith, I cried out.

One week later, my dad came home, asking for help. He had me mix him a drink (it was certainly the weakest drink in human history). Then, I called Mom, who called a family friend, Swede, who was active in Alcoholics Anonymous. Swede came over. Later that week, my dad went into rehab for 28 days. He came home on Thanksgiving Day.

I began searching to know this God who had answered a teen's desperate cry. I was tired of hiding the shame and unworthiness I felt. I was tired of the chaos and my own anger at everyone and everything around me.

A friend on the Junior Varsity football team invited me to a beach trip with his church youth group. I loved that church. That's where I met Cherie. She was a Junior (swoon) and a redhead (double swoon). We dated for a month, and by that time, I was building relationships in the church. I sang in the youth choir and played basketball, football, and softball with the associate pastors of the church, both of whom were good athletes.

I read *I Am Third,* by Gale Sayers, the Hall of Fame running back for the Chicago Bears. He wrote that his source of joy was Jesus first, Others second, Yourself third (J. O. Y.). I also read *The Cross and the Switchblade,* by Pastor David Wilkerson. Years before, he had begun an outreach for addicted and violent teens and young adults called *Teen Challenge,* located in Bedford-Stuyvesant in New York City. Wilkerson had helped lead a gang leader named Nicky Cruz to faith in Jesus. (Cruz initially came to one of the meetings to kill Wilkerson.)

All this time, I was certain the problems I experienced in life were not my problems. They were somebody else's problems. The problems were my parents' drinking, my mom's rage, and my geometry teacher's inability to give me a good grade. My problem was the other boys in class with whom I fought.

Throughout this time of searching, I experienced periods of deep depression. I thought about how I might end the emotional suffering I felt - believing the whole time that it all came from outside of me.

But the core of my turmoil had been spoken to me at that sweltering Friday night football game: "Loomis, you have a problem!"

I finally began to understand that I was broken by the effects of sin. *The Lord observed the extent of human wickedness on the earth, and he saw that everything they thought or imagined was consistently and totally evil.* (Genesis 6:5 NLT) And I learned that this was still true for all people – including me. Much later, the prophet Jeremiah wrote in the book of Jeremiah, chapter 17: *The human heart is the most deceitful of all things, and desperately wicked.* (v 9 NLT)

Maybe it was the words or actions of others that started a process in me leading to anger, fear, and bitterness, but I was the one who harbored that anger, nursed those grudges, and chose bitterness.

Above all, I could not fix myself. I was sick and needed a healer. I was drowning in anger and shame and needed a Savior. I was hiding from God and needed to know that I was so loved and precious that God the Father willingly chose to send his one and only Son, Jesus, to die on a cross so I might be saved from sin and the grave and healed from their power over me.

I could do nothing. It was not in my power to fix, heal, or save myself. I soon came to understand that my salvation was a gift – from God himself. It was offered without a cost to me. All I needed to do was to receive God's gift, which made me sorry for my sin and anger and fear; gave me the power to offer my sin and shortcomings to God so that He could do what only God can do: take the sin off my shoulders and nail it to the cross of Jesus; then throw it away.

Jesus, in the Gospel written by His follower John, shines the spotlight best in chapter 3, verses 16-17: *For this is how God loved the world: He gave his one and only Son, so that everyone who believes in him will not perish but have eternal life. God sent his Son into the world not to judge the world, but to save the world through him.* (NLT)

In 1970, David Wilkerson came to town. That night, as he shared the good news about Jesus Christ – His love and forgiveness, His resurrection and salvation – I went forward at the Bayfront Center in downtown St. Petersburg, where I said "Yes" to Jesus. I asked for forgiveness for my sin, for all the things I could think of I had done wrong. I asked Jesus to clean my life up, heal me, and help me live for Him.

Tired of the chaos and the anger, hungering for the God who cared enough to save my dad and who might just possibly love me, I turned to Jesus, now convinced that He was the One I was searching for.

My search for God did not end at that point. It shifted gears.

I wanted to know everything about Jesus. I wanted to know *Him.* I read the Bible, especially the four biographies of Jesus (called the Gospels). I went to the Bible studies that our church offered for teens. Later that year, I went to a prayer and worship group on Tuesday nights at a neighboring church.

As important as studying the Bible was, I also spent a lot of time with people who were further along in their life of faith than I was. I started to listen to the messages by the two pastors at my church (rather than just passing notes to girls during the sermon). I spent a lot of time with a college-aged guy from that Tuesday night prayer and worship time. Rich had a joy and a peace that I wanted. His mentoring helped me discover how I could have that, too.

Through time in worship, prayer, the Scriptures, and these relationships, I began to experience the peace and joy I had longed for.

Even though God was healing me, I was (and still am) far from perfect. I was still angry. Maybe because I had never experienced any other way of living, I still felt like my life was chaotic.

I came to learn that the healing of our spirits is often like the healing of our bodies - some illnesses or injuries take time. And my healing continued as the Holy Spirit worked in me.

I learned God wanted more for me than to simply get me into heaven. He wanted to get heaven into me. He wanted me to experience a new way of living. In fact, Jesus taught that we have a spiritual enemy (sometimes called the devil; in this verse, the thief) when he said, *The thief's purpose is to steal and kill and destroy. My purpose is to give them a rich and satisfying life.* (John 10:10 NLT)

One of my breakthroughs came when I realized some things about my parents. Much of my anger was due to my childhood understanding of all that had gone on in our family. I blamed my parents for the chaos and emotional pain that I experienced.

As an adult, I began to do some genealogy work. I discovered that my mom's dad was an alcoholic. He died when she was two years old - from alcoholism (his death certificate lists his cause of death as "alcoholism related to moonshine"). My mom was the fourth of five children, and the only girl. During the Great Depression, things were very hard for her and her family. All that was made worse by not having a father.

My dad's father died when dad was 15. He was coming home from a bar, drunk, in the winter. He fell into a snowdrift and froze to death.

Once again, in the words of that classmate from long ago, "Loomis, you have a problem!"

The problem wasn't 'them.' It wasn't anyone or anything else. I had the problem. It was my anger, my sin, my bitterness, my choices.

All of this helped me to realize that my parents never intended to harm anyone. They were doing the best they knew how to do. The result was that I was able to forgive them for the wrongs I blamed them for. As a result, I learned something about the forgiveness of God. When we forgive, we experience the healing power of forgiveness. As Jesus said, *"If you forgive those who sin against you, your heavenly Father will forgive you. But if you refuse to forgive others, your Father will not forgive your sins."* (Matthew 6:14-15 NLT)

The Holy Spirit continued to work in me, healing me.

At about the same time, I heard God's voice. I had been angry at someone who had hurt me, and while I was sitting in a concert at church, one of the singers said something that stirred the embers of anger in me toward that individual again. That is when I heard God speak. It was not an audible voice like you would hear from another person. I can only describe it as a very strong impression in my mind. But I knew that it was God.

He said, "Mike, what right do you have to be offended?"

I knew immediately what that meant. Jesus died on the cross for my sin and the sin of everyone in the world. Yet, He chose to forgive rather than to be offended. He was executed by those He came to save. Yet, He said, *"Father, forgive them for they don't know what they are doing,"* (Luke 23:34 NLT) rather than, "Father, make sure they burn in hell for this."

I understood at that moment that the world has done far more to Jesus than it will ever do to me. If the Son of God who came to save and heal me could forgive those who crucified Him, what right do I have to be offended? Ever!? Once again, I realized that the problem was not outside of me. I had the problem. I needed healing and help.

I have come to understand that I am most open to God when I am most desperate.

It was when I was desperate for God's wisdom that I fought to spend time in Scripture.

It was when I was desperate for God's help that I disciplined myself to pray.

It was when I desperately needed to grow that I sought out companions who would help me stay on the journey with Jesus.

Spending time with Jesus in the Bible and in prayer puts us in a place where the Holy Spirit can transform us. Paul, a great teacher of the faith, put it like this: *Anyone who belongs to Christ has become a new person. The old life is gone; a new life has begun!* (2 Corinthians 5:17, NLT)

Each day, Jesus is picking up the broken pieces and, bit by bit, healing me.

Each season of my life, He has provided men of honor, integrity, and grace.

I belong to Jesus. A new life has begun.

SEAN LOOMIS

Sean was born and raised in Florida. He, his wife April, and their three children—Lydia, Juniper, and Baby TBD—live in Royal Palm Beach. Sean and April have a fulfilling marriage and fulfilling careers.

As a pastor's kid, Sean grew up in the church. He gave his life to Jesus at the age of 10 at a Christian Youth Camp. He graduated from Palm Beach Atlantic University in 2007 with a degree in Ministry and Leadership.

Sean settled in Palm Beach County, where he decided to go into worship and pastoral ministry and later transitioned into the business world through Financial Services. His full-time vocation is in Biblical Financial Coaching, but his heart is ministering to those in need of salvation and redemption through deliverance and discipleship. His favorite Bible verse is 1 Peter 3:15. *Always be ready to give a...reason for the hope that is in you.* (NKJV)

THERE IS PURPOSE IN THE PAIN

BY SEAN LOOMIS

The marriage was over. Our little family was broken, and our 2-year-old had divorced parents. My time in ministry as a pastor was done. I was being forced against my will to leave my career, my calling, and any comfort I had. I was angry and depressed. I was overwhelmed with fear. I was soon to be financially ruined and, shortly thereafter, would develop an auto-immune disease.

"You're going into the wilderness," I heard inside my mind and felt it in my spirit as clearly as someone telling me to my face.

Up to this point—in my early 30s—I spent most of my life avoiding pain and fears and not confronting my sin or dealing with the reality of broken relationships in my life. I worked in full-time ministry as a worship pastor, and although I also did marriage counseling and premarital counseling, my own marriage was in a bad place from early on. I brought unresolved sin into the marriage, she had wounds and brokenness she didn't want to talk about, and we could not communicate. I wanted to find counseling, but I alone desired to seek help.

She told me she would divorce me if I told anyone about our problems or struggles. So I chose to live in fear of the consequences of seeking help for our marriage. I kept our problems hidden, knowing I was being disobedient to God. I hoped and prayed God would do something in that marriage, but I didn't take control of my life and wasn't willing to accept the consequences that being open and honest would bring. Feeling depressed and like everything wrong in our relationship was my fault, I pretended to the world that everything was OK.

Less than five years into the marriage, my worst fears came true, and the stress and sense of failure came in like a flood. It all disintegrated, and there was nothing in my world to which I could cling. All the little decisions I made along the way to avoid pain and consequences or hide what was going on, pretending everything was fine, caught up to me. I kept hoping a miracle would happen in that relationship, but nothing changed, and the divorce was finalized.

I didn't just lose the marriage; I also lost my family and my full-time ministry. And I thought I had lost my calling. All I could do was submit and cling to God. My will had been to keep the status quo moving in the same direction. I didn't want to deviate from whatever comfortable path I was on. I wanted to maintain my life as it was. But it was not to be.

Better is the end of a thing than its beginning; the patient in spirit are better than the proud in spirit... Say not, "Why were the former days better than these?" For it is not from wisdom that you ask this... Consider the work of God; who can make straight what he has made crooked? In the day of prosperity be joyful, and in the day of adversity consider; God has made the one as well as the other, so that man may not find out anything that will be after him. (Ecclesiastes 7:8, 10, 13-14 ESV)

I was certainly in "the day of adversity," and since, I have "considered"— asking myself what led up to all of this.

I would say that I've been afraid most of my life. From childhood to my early 30s, fear kept me from living up to my potential. I was afraid of failing and succeeding. I was afraid of people knowing who I was deep inside. And I was afraid to confront fear itself!

I grew up in a Christian home full of music, singing, joy, and laughter. It's hard to say when the seeds of fear and self-doubt were planted in my early childhood. I believe it could have only been the devil's influence. I had a good family with loving and intentional parents who sought to give us a good life.

I didn't experience abuse or tragedy; however, I often felt frustration and fear that I would never be good enough. I felt inadequate—like I would never measure up. Yes, I was short! Maybe I didn't measure up in my mind because I was a physically small kid, leading me to also feel like a small person.

The enemy of our souls works hard to plant seeds of doubt and destruction at a very young age so that we will struggle throughout our lives.

> There is no fear in love, but perfect love casts out fear. For fear has to do with punishment, and whoever fears has not been perfected in love. (1 John 4:18 ESV)

I was ten years old when I went away to a Christian youth camp. Sitting in the chapel night after night, I heard the preachers talking about the perfect love of God and the need for a sinless Savior. Even at that young age, I felt so much angst and confusion. I knew deep down I needed someone to save me from sin and death. I couldn't save myself. So I went forward to the altar and committed my heart and life to Jesus. And yet, I still had not learned to receive God's perfect love in every area of my life.

As afraid as I was of facing certain aspects of life, I've never been afraid of death. When I became a Christian, I told myself I would die for my faith in Jesus. In my teenage years, I distinctly remember hearing God say, "Sean, you would die for your faith, but would you truly live for your faith?" Living in the abundant life Jesus provides is a daily sacrifice I had to learn to make. It's a sacrifice I would eventually learn to make after the divorce.

When I was a teenager, my dad came to our youth group and shared his testimony of how he came to faith. It radically changed my view of him. Because of his testimony, I fell more in love with God as my heavenly Father and committed myself all the more to Jesus. My dad chose to face a lot of his childhood trauma and sacrificed so much so that we could have a better life. He overcame a lot of his fears. He is the most impactful man I've ever known. He wasn't a perfect man, but he was the perfect father for us; he certainly strived to be a man of integrity and honor.

Because of my father's example, my parent's marriage, and my own desire to be married and have my own family, I never thought I would be the guy to get divorced. I said that would never be me. And so, with the divorce, every part of me was painted with failure.

"Sean, you're going into the wilderness. My Spirit led Jesus into the wilderness, and Jesus chose to go. I'll walk with you through it. It's time to GO!" God was speaking. I was listening, but I didn't wanna go anywhere. I just wanted to lie down and give up. But God told me to go. Leave the church, the career, the ministry, and the life I knew.

So I decided I needed to step down as a worship pastor. I was no longer worthy of the calling placed on my life.

In the wilderness, the devil attempted to take Jesus off course. Jesus was in the most vulnerable place He would ever be except when He fulfilled His mission on the cross. The enemy tried to manipulate the truth and tried to deceive Jesus. The enemy attacked Jesus' calling to save the world, His physical weakness as a human being, and His identity as the Son of God.

The prophet Isaiah wrote about Jesus identifying with our broken humanity hundreds of years before.

> *He was despised and rejected by men, a man of sorrows and acquainted with grief; and as one from whom men hide their faces he was despised, and we esteemed him not. Surely he has borne our griefs and carried our sorrows; yet we esteemed him stricken, smitten by God, and afflicted. But he was pierced for our transgressions; he was crushed for our iniquities; upon him was the chastisement that brought us peace, and with his wounds we are healed.* (Isaiah 53:3-5 ESV)

Jesus knew His identity. And He didn't waiver. The devil had been hitting me hard regarding my calling and my identity. Things were about to get worse, but God was always present and guiding me.

God started bringing people into my life to keep me going. A guy from the church named Jerry kept reaching out to me. I wasn't good friends with him at the time. I had briefly helped him in my time as a pastor. However, I didn't know why he cared or kept asking me to spend time with him and his wife and family. But I kept hearing that voice of God say, "If someone invites you, GO!"

Jerry was an honorable man to his wife and children. They would invite my daughter and me to the beach or on camping trips, and I would hear the Spirit say, "GO!" I would go simply out of obedience to God, knowing He didn't want me to isolate.

I also didn't want to attend church, as I was bitter about leaving my previous church ministry. But I did find some healing in a home church. I am usually an extreme extrovert, but I didn't want to be around people. Still, I kept forcing myself to go. I kept being obedient to what I thought God told me to do in the wilderness.

It took me a while to allow God to work on me during that wilderness season. Failure was my identity, and stress became my way of life. I was so stressed that I started dying inside. It all didn't make sense. I grew up in the church, was a pastor's kid, loved God, cared about people, and had a personal relationship with Jesus. I knew in my head that He loved me, I knew in my mind God had a plan for me, but my heart and emotions were totally shot. I began to physically waste away.

The chronic stress caused me to develop an auto-immune disease. This disease is called Ulcerative Colitis. Basically, my body couldn't process food because my stomach and colon could not absorb nutrients. This particular disease caused internal bleeding in my colon. This was not just a stomach ulcer—I was bleeding out so badly that, over the course of a year, my body couldn't sustain the blood loss. I was using the restroom 30-40 times daily, and (I apologize for the graphic pictures) only blood came out of me. I lost 30+ pounds, four waist sizes, and I couldn't absorb nutrients anymore. I had a 0% BMI. My body was eating itself to death.

When I understood what was happening physically, it became clear why I had cognitive issues. I struggled to regulate my emotions because my hormones were off, and I had severe brain fog and memory loss. I couldn't think straight. Physically and mentally, I was wasting away.

I was also struggling to work and make an income. My employer had also been through a divorce and, subsequently, developed Ulcerative Colitis, so understanding what I was going through, he kept paying me. That was a small miracle. Still, in an attempt to maintain the same lifestyle I had when I was married, I made bad financial decisions and lost everything. The good news is that, because of the divorce, I didn't have much anyways.

Finally, after months of severe decline, I went to the gastroenterologist and got an official diagnosis. The doctor told me I would eventually get cancer, needed to have my colon removed, and my kidneys would eventually fail due to the medicine I was taking. Oh, and I would be on dialysis by my late 30s.

I sat across from the doctor with my dad by my side, listening to the dismal diagnosis. Intense fear and anger washed over me, and I heard the voice in my head saying that this was how I would die; this was how I would be remembered—broken and destroyed.

Jesus says in John 10:10, *The thief comes to steal, kill, and destroy. I have come that they may have life and have it abundantly.* (ESV) I had let the enemy steal so many years of my life. I even let him convince me that death was better than life.

In that moment, I started speaking to my spirit. "No, this is not how I'm going to die. Everything that's coming out of this doctor's mouth is a lie. I'm not going to let this take me down." I felt righteous anger inside of me. I knew that God had a plan and purpose for my life. Deep down, I believed He had a future for me, and I began to hope. I believed there was a better way to live, and I wouldn't let a diagnosis dictate how I lived the rest of my life.

I seemed to have lost my identity, calling, and health, but God was shifting my perspective.

In the coming days, I started pushing through the fear. I began to pray God would help me take authority over my life, including my health, finances, and, of course, fear itself. And I saw God do many miracles in response. Too many to even share in this short memoir.

After my diagnosis, I started doing a lot of research. First, I called the founder of the world's most successful supplement company (whom I met through church many years before) and asked him what I should do to get healthy. He had overcome cancer and Crohn's disease, and he shared with me his wisdom, which I followed 100%, beginning my miraculous health journey.

Sometimes I felt like John the Baptist, eating weird things that didn't always taste so good. But God answered my prayers regarding my health. It took about nine months to recognize the difference. Proverbs 24:3 says, *By wisdom a house is built, and by understanding it is established.* (ESV) God gave me the miracle of wisdom to rebuild my temple—the house of the Holy Spirit.

And there were plenty of other miracles along the way.

I had another acquaintance whom I would occasionally reach out to because he and his wife did counseling and relationship coaching. His name is Brian. He invited me to his home to teach me how to take control of my finances. I heard God say, "GO!"

Brian was an honorable man. One day, before I had seen any results from my healthy choices, I drove to his house after work feeling terrible. In fact, I felt sicker and lower than ever, and I thought, "I'll just go home and go to bed, and I hope I never wake up." I wanted to die rather than endure the pain. But the Spirit inside me kept saying, "Go to Brian's. You've been praying out about this." So again, I decided to be obedient.

As a financial coach, Brian helped me put together a financial game plan. He showed me how to take control of my finances, and he walked through life with me. He taught me how to get out of debt and prepare for the future. And Brian introduced me to another honorable businessman, Kenny. Kenny was one of the most positive people I had ever met.

I continued to meet other leaders and business mentors who became friends. They inspired me with their stories of victory, and I decided to use my testimony of financial brokenness to help others with their finances.

My new step into the financial world was scary. I was still overcoming health challenges and had no idea how to help myself, let alone help others. But God provided a way forward. I became educated and earned my financial licenses so I could help others. I was willing, and I heeded His call. I have since sat with hundreds of people, teaching them how to take control of their finances and build wealth. More importantly, as a result of my obedience, many have come to know Jesus through my coaching.

Through my fear, God gave me a testimony in all the broken areas of my life—health, finances, and my calling.

My business mentors and leaders also opened my eyes to the spiritual battle going on inside and around me by introducing me to the Band of Brothers men's ministry. They kept inviting me into their world. They weren't afraid of the mess I was in. With them, I could be real, raw, and authentic and never feel judged or ashamed of my past or what I was struggling with.

Kenny also held a Bible Study at his house. At this time, I was still very sick and wanted to isolate myself. So initially, I wasn't sure I wanted to go. But reluctantly, I went, and one Sunday at Bible Study, after several years of struggling and nine months of pursuing health, financial wellness, and showing up where God called, I met my future wife, April.

We now have three beautiful children. And that guy Jerry? He became one of my best friends and the best man at our wedding. He also became one of the very first people I helped with his finances!

I believe God is always speaking. He is always wanting to move on our behalf. And He is always near to us, especially when we are broken-hearted. God truly does have a purpose for our pain and gives us a plan for the future.

O Lord my God, I cried to you for help, and you have healed me. (Psalm 30:2 ESV)

FAITH TO OVERCOME SHAME

Shame puts out a message. Are you plagued with shame's message, questioning, "Am I a bad person for what I did?" or maybe, "Was it me who did something wrong?" Are you struggling, trying to throw off the weight shame dispenses in your life?

In its various forms, shame identifies us as unacceptable, dirty, and disgraced. It comes upon people differently, but its root is always in sin.

Guilt and shame are often left in sin's wake, even after forgiveness has been sought and granted. Shame says, "I will never let anyone do this to me ever again, so I will build walls." While guilt says, "What did I do to warrant this? I must have done something to deserve this."

We can feel shame because we were wronged. Sadly, this is common in abuse victims, covered by deep hurt and pain. Verbal abuse, physical abuse, neglect, sexual abuse, and trauma can all result in a struggle for worthiness.

Sometimes we hang shame on others. We hide and protect ourselves while we accuse someone else, causing them undue harm. And sometimes, we refuse to release others from shame by being unforgiving when they have wronged us.

The tragedy of shame is that it can take us off mission, cause us to continue sinning, and make us want to isolate ourselves. This gives the enemy his way in our minds and leads to self-medications of escape.

But God's ways are always higher than our ways, and what threatens to defeat us, He has the power to conquer. God is Holy and perfectly pure; He alone is the One who is able to overcome the contamination and residue of sin and shame. Our Savior's way is to act on our behalf and take our shame from us. He does not ignore sin, but He brings forward grace and truth to us. How does He do this?

When shame rises from the root of sin, understand that Jesus has nailed our sins to the cross, and they no longer have power over us. It is one thing to believe our sin has been removed, but another to KNOW that there is a divine love that can NEVER be removed, no matter what we have done. Jesus says, *"Take heart, son; your sins are forgiven"* (Matthew 9:2 NIV) Sometimes we are the forgiven, and sometimes we are to be the forgivers. Whichever shame you are carrying, God can release you.

Unreleased shame hinders us in many ways. It can hinder you and prevent you from finding your purpose. Shame can hinder you from working your purpose-driven career. Shame brings insecurities that can hold you back from fulfilling what God has gifted and equipped you to do. Shame hinders relationships from thriving—causing us to shut down emotionally as we seek protection due to past fears and experiences. Shame can cause feelings of ongoing hurt in areas we have no control over anymore. God knows the truth about whatever has happened in your past, and He can stop the chaotic spiral of shaming.

Shame and guilt disappear in a relationship with Jesus. God's truth is good news for us, even though it means consequences for sin. God does not ignore sin, pretending it is not there or not bad. Instead, He warns us what sin leads to. Shame leads us to hide from the truth and not expose the evil. You can be assured that God knows your situation, He has seen exactly what happened, and He will not draw you into fear or chaos over it as He heals you. He will lead you to truth and honesty with grace, whatever the situation is, and He will bring you to freedom. By the power of the cross, shame is already defeated.

Great news, your faith in Christ heals you from shame and brings complete freedom. Jesus' mission on earth was to set the captives free—and that includes freedom from the prison of shame. God does not give you over to shame's lie that says your sin is hopeless and all-encompassing with no solution. God's promise of triumph is a promise to work through one who is unworthy. Christ is the Victor who overcame sin and shame, and He can accomplish His work for His glory.

We are all sinful and shameful people. Jesus' blood covers our sins. Remember to reflect truth that God is not ashamed of us. Jesus died for sin and shame. It takes tremendous faith and courage to walk away from any form of shame and refocus on the praise from Almighty God.

> Instead of your shame you will receive a double portion, and instead of disgrace you will rejoice in your inheritance. And so, you will inherit a double portion in your land, and everlasting joy will be yours. (Isaiah 61:7 NIV)

Do not allow your own self-evaluation or that of others to set your mind off course. Strive to be a great Man of Honor who overcomes shame through faith in Jesus Christ. Look to God's Word for your help. 1 Corinthians 4:1-13 may help you to name the shame. Once you identify your shame, nail it to the cross for the last time. You can then move on to freedom in Christ alone. With Him, you will find true inner peace and immense joy.

. . . .

JULIO SOTO

Julio Soto was born in the borough of Manhattan, in the city of New York and raised by two loving parents (an Irish mom who was a schoolteacher and a Puerto Rican dad who was a business owner) with three sisters in a loving, middle-class environment. His family moved to The Bronx when he was ten. A true New Yorker, he lived in Queens and Long Island before moving to Tampa, Florida, with his wife, Lina. He has two awesome children: a daughter and a son, whom he loves dearly.

Julio's hobbies are sports (he played baseball in college), reading, and spending time with his wife. His passion is to help people 1) Honor God, 2) Pursue excellence, 3) and become leaders. He and his wife lead a team of amazing people in the financial services arena. He can be contacted at www.livemore.net/Sotojr or teamusa.soto7@gmail.com

FROM SINNER, TO SAVED; TO SINNER; TO FORGIVEN.

BY JULIO SOTO

The enemy has a toolbox of spiritual tactics that he uses against believers, and becoming a Christian doesn't automatically make a person fully aware of them. Likewise, having moral laws encoded into our hearts by the Holy Spirit makes us understand the difference between right and wrong but doesn't automatically make us immune to the devils' tactics.

I believed in God my entire life. And I was surrounded by Christian influences as far back as I can remember. I went to Catholic school in 1st and 4th grade, and one of my lifelong friends was heavily involved in his faith. In fact, he later became a pastor. I verbally accepted Christ as my Lord and Savior when I was about 30 years old after attending a Christian event with that same friend. He convinced me to go to the event by telling me there would be a softball tournament. Since I played college baseball, he knew that would draw me. He was right. Although I didn't verbally accept Christ as my Lord and Savior at that event, it left a powerful and lasting impression that ultimately led me to do so several years later.

I fully accepted Jesus Christ as my Savior during my *first* marriage.

I always thought that once I got married, I would never divorce. My parents divorced when I was 16, and it was one of the most painful and difficult things I experienced as a teenager. I didn't want to repeat the trend. I promised myself I never would. But the enemy didn't care what I had promised-to myself or anyone else - and my eyes weren't fully aware of his schemes or plans. I must have "conveniently forgotten" that I promised myself I would never divorce. Instead, I convinced myself I wasn't "in love" and looked for a way to annul the marriage after only a few months. I was sure I had all the right "reasons" for wanting to end the marriage. *But excuses are just alibis disguised as reasons.*

Then I got the news: I'm gonna be a dad. I can remember my wife telling me with trepidation that she was pregnant. I believe she was afraid I'd be upset. She knew things were not going well with us and didn't want to disappoint me with the news we were having a baby. As strange as this may sound, the news did not upset me. That's not to say I wasn't nervous, because I was. But I was also excited to become a dad. Unfortunately, instead of committing to being a good husband and dad, for the next five years I played the part of an "apathetic-bachelor- husband." In other words, I didn't live respecting the sanctity of marriage. I didn't aggressively pursue other women, but I sure did passively. I wasn't the physically absent husband, always out with friends, spending little time with my wife. But I was emotionally absent. The time we spent together could not have been considered quality time either. You can sometimes be in the same room with a person and still be miles apart. You can be respectful with someone but disrespect the relationship in a myriad of other ways. I was going through the motions. I'm sure you know exactly what I'm talking about. I never went the extra mile to be anything resembling a model husband. In all transparency, my behavior as a Christian man was anything but Christ-like! If I had to use a word to describe my behavior, that word would be *hypocrite*. Here I was, claiming to be a Christian, yet sinning against my wife and against God. I looked at other women with desire. Sometimes I did more than look. Then I returned home, and with those same eyes that strayed lustfully, I would look at my wife, portraying that everything was ok. I hid my hypocrisy behind the façade of a "good guy." Hypocrite was too nice a word to describe me.

Unfortunately, this behavior didn't stop when my daughter came into the world. And I don't believe I have ever loved someone the way I have loved my daughter (I call her my 1st love). But did that stop my behavior? No! And because it did not, my behavior progressively became worse and worse. I figured that since I didn't have the courage (which in retrospect was really cowardice in disguise) to ask for a divorce (which I knew was something God did not want me to do), then I might as well allow my bad behavior to progress. Which I did. As you can imagine, this caused tremendous pain for my wife and daughter. Neither of whom deserved it at all. I inflicted terrible wounds on two people I love. I do not have the words to describe the remorse and guilt that followed me.

I call those days my "Dark Ages." I don't remember much about them other than the guilt I had and the wounds, pain, and hurt I caused to my ex-wife (we divorced after five years) and my first love, my one and only daughter. My Babygirl.

Let's fast forward several years. I'm divorced (broken promises). I find myself in a relationship with another woman-promising myself not to marry again because "been there; done that." And "don't want to go through that again!" This relationship, with a beautiful woman of God, lasted several years. She was great, but I didn't want to get married, and she did. So, what did I do? Yep! You guessed it! I ended up getting married a second time after five years of being with her.

It's difficult to say which divorce was more gut-wrenching or devastating. In any case, the second divorce was no less hypocritical than the first. Perhaps it was even more distressing because I was more actively seeking and pursuing God during this time. But that didn't stop me from having an affair. An affair that resulted in my second divorce. An affair that had me professing Christ with my mouth but rejecting Him with my actions. This, obviously, caused even more guilt and shame.

Here's the thing about guilt and shame: it gives you a feeling that it's ok to continue to do wrong because you'll always feel you're never good enough or worthy enough for forgiveness. So, you continue to sin, which is what I did. This affair also caused an overwhelming fear. Fear that I would be exposed as a hypocrite yet again. No one wants to be exposed as a hypocrite. No one wants to be discovered as an imposter. But that is exactly what I was! An imposter! A hypocrite! The epitome of a "Poser." I was professing Christianity yet living a lie, which led to my second divorce.

The crushing thing about divorce is that in most cases it doesn't mean a separation only from a spouse, it also means separation from your children. This was the case again for me in this second divorce from my second wife – and second child. My son. This time my hurt went even deeper - because the love for my son was too great to describe. I was left with a provocative question, a question to which the answer haunted me for years. That question was this: *What can a man who's been divorced two times ever teach his children about love and marriage?* For me then, the answer was nothing. Absolutely nothing!

Two divorces later, two broken marriages. Five broken hearts. A broken man. The casualties of my selfishness, ego, infidelity, and the list goes on. I don't have the vocabulary to describe to you the intense guilt I lived with. I was an emotional wreck-dying a slow death of remorse. The enemy is a master at using guilt.

During the broken months that followed I attended a men's event that changed my life, an event that has had the greatest impact in more ways than I can describe. I'd known about this event - this "Band of Brothers' Bootcamp" - for years. I had always wanted to attend one. But invariably, something always "came up." I'm convinced the enemy knew this and worked overtime to keep me from this event. I believe if I had attended this Men's Bootcamp during my first marriage, I would have never divorced. Ignorance isn't bliss.

My girlfriend, who would become my third wife, knew I wanted to attend the Bootcamp. So, she got it for me as a Christmas gift. Other than my salvation, my kids, and my current wife, this was one of the greatest gifts I'd ever receive. The Bootcamp changed my life in more ways than I can say. Attending it reminded me of the truth. And that truth set me, a captive of guilt and shame, free. Finding the truth gifted me with what I desperately needed - PEACE. I had finally become a Man of Honor.

> *Then you will know the truth, and the truth will set you free.* (John 8:32 NIV)

During one session, we had "QUIET TIME" when we were given a sheet of paper with some questions. I took the paper, walked behind a building, and placed my chair facing the trees and the forest. The sun was bright, and the breeze was beautiful. I was totally emotional. I read one question.

"God, what are you up to? What are you after?"

Now listen to me. I'm not gonna sit here and tell you that at that moment, the clouds parted, a bright light shone down on me, and a thunderous voice spoke through those clouds, but I'm telling you, I heard God's voice as loud as thunder in my mind.

The moment I read the question, I heard God IMMEDIATELY say to me:

"YOUR PEACE!" He was after my Peace!

At that moment, a butterfly flew directly in front of me. The only butterfly I saw that whole week. It was as if God was telling me:

"I forgive you! This moment you are reborn. Can't you see me? I free you from your guilt. And I still love you."

I totally lost it right there. Completely overwhelmed with emotion. And with relief.

> For this is what the high and exalted One says—He who lives forever, whose name is holy:"I live in a high and holy place, but also with the one who is contrite and lowly in spirit, to revive the spirit of the lowly and to revive the heart of the contrite. I will not accuse them forever, nor will I always be angry, for then they would faint away because of me— the very people I have created." (Isaiah 57:15-16 NIV)

God had me right where He wanted me! He was chasing me down the entire time during my failures, weaknesses, and sins. And at my lowest point, when I was living with a broken spirit and a contrite heart, He spoke to me with His truth...

> My sacrifice, O God, is a broken spirit; a broken and contrite heart you, God, will not despise. (Psalm 51:17 NIV)

Jesus was chasing after me. He knew I needed healing.

> "The Spirit of the Lord is upon Me (the Messiah), Because He has anointed Me to preach the good news to the poor. He has sent Me to announce release (pardon, forgiveness) to the captives, and recovery of sight to the blind, to set free those who are oppressed (downtrodden, bruised, crushed by tragedy)." (Luke 4:18 AMP)

I needed to be at that Bootcamp. Because of my guilt and shame, I felt unworthy of happiness and success. My spirit was ready. I was remorseful and prostrate with humility, begging for God to help me.

> "Has not my hand made all these things, and so they came into being?" declares the Lord. "These are the ones I look on with favor: those who are humble and contrite in spirit, and who tremble at my word." (Isaiah 66:2 NIV)

I believe that guilt and isolation are some of the most effective tools the enemy uses to keep people from living an abundant, free life. He uses these weapons in tandem, knowing that if he can make men feel guilty enough, they will isolate themselves from an environment that will bless them. And he will do everything in his power to make that happen. He will convince powerful people they are not powerful, and worthy people they are not worthy. The devil will go out of his way to make those with a strong work ethic believe they are too busy or lazy, or that they shouldn't work so hard to do what God has called them to do. He persuades capable people that they do not have what it takes to win. The bottom line is that the devil knows if he can get a powerful, worthy, strong, hungry, and capable man or woman of God away from other like-minded warriors, he will win the battle.

I learned quite a few lessons at that Bootcamp. Here are just a few of them:

1. The enemy cannot destroy God, so he seeks to destroy God's image—us.

2. We cannot be what God wants us to be by pretending to be someone else. If we are "posing" (putting up a front of someone we are not, living a lie).

3. The enemy is a master at using guilt and distortion to destroy us.

4. The worse our sin (our story) is, the more God can use us.

5. The more we resist temptation, the *more* power we have. And our power is not conquering the world, or women. Instead, our power lies in conquering our temptations and allowing the love of Christ to conquer *us*.

During those two divorces, I lost the battles. But with my eyes opened wide, fully aware that the enemy was real and in attack mode, and with Christ by my side, I won the war. Even as Christians we still have battles, but when we keep God by our side, we win a ton more than we lose. A ton.

But this is not the best part of my failures. Before I was set free, before I found the peace I so desperately needed, I was a man who professed Christianity hypocritically. After I discovered the truth, and the love of God rescued me from my burden, *I went from professing Christianity to possessing Christianity.*

My relationship now with my third and final wife (whew) could not be stronger. We both pursue God with all our hearts, and we pursue each other with that same love. We are both connected to each other and to Christ as ONE. What the enemy meant for evil; God will turn for good if you allow Him. I am free now!

Yes, the battles continue. We still must fight them. But we know how the war ends. So does the enemy. We know how to fight alongside God and other Christians, other men of honor. And our weapons for this spiritual war are simple. And today there isn't a day that goes by where we don't wield those weapons. This is how we fight our battles: with prayer, staying in the Word (reading my bible), and listening to worship music. Hallelujah.

RON SETRAN

Ron Setran currently serves as the COO for Prayer Stations Inc. He is also a certified financial coach, runs a web development company—Precise Technology Solutions, a texting service—OneTeamText, and was previously the Director of IT for a health club in Westchester, New York.

Ron has had the opportunity to run basketball clinics in southern Thailand, sit on the edge of a 2,000 ft cliff in Norway, play dodgeball with kids at a juvenile detention center in Estonia, enjoy amazing seafood at a family-owned restaurant in Sicily, visit the Panama Canal, walk up a waterfall in Jamaica, play in a jazz band for the Vice President, be at Game 6 of the 1986 World Series (Bill Buckner!), marry the love of his life, and have three amazing children. And that is just a taste.

Ron Setran - ronsetran@protonmail.com

BRIAN,

YOU HAVE BECOME ONE OF MY GOOD FRIENDS AND APPRECIATE AND VALUE YOU BRIAN. I LOOK FORWARD TO ALL GOD HAS FOR YOU AND YOUR FUTURE. WISHING YOU ALL THE BEST!

1 PETER 3:15

THE VALUE OF A BREATH

BY RON SETRAN

When my wife, Anita, and I first heard about COVID, we had no idea just how much it would change our and our family's lives forever. But looking back to see God's hand in all of it - I can't wait to tell you the story.

First, let me give you some background. I was born and raised in a strict Christian household in Smithtown, New York. I became a youth volunteer for the church's youth group, where I met my future wife, Anita. She grew up in a missionary family, living and traveling the world over. Her parents were well-known evangelists who were a part of an organization called *Youth With A Mission* (YWAM) since the early 1970s.

Anita and I met in 1991 and were married less than a year later. We have experienced life in a way few others have while living a life of missions, including the opportunity to travel around the world. In addition, God blessed us with three amazing kids: Caleb is now 24 and married to his beautiful wife Diana, Karissa is 22, and our youngest, Kiersten, is 18.

Our first encounter with COVID began when our daughter, Karissa, tested COVID-positive in early July 2021. We took care of her with the limited knowledge we had at the time. Then, our other two kids and Anita and I tested positive in mid-August 2021.

While our kids recovered relatively quickly, Anita and I had quite a different experience. As each day passed, my breathing became more and more labored. Sleeping was almost impossible as it felt like a massive weight had been placed on my lungs and I became very short of breath. I began to wonder what the endpoint would be to my story.

Although we were under the care of our general practitioner, our symptoms were escalating. It was recommended that we get checked at a local hospital, so we had our daughter drive us. We were grateful to be placed in the same room in the emergency room (ER). A doctor came in, and one of the first questions he asked was our vaccination status. Upon hearing we were not vaccinated, there was an instantaneous change in his communication style. Anita and I both had chest X-rays, and a few minutes later, the doctor came back to say that I had the beginning stages of COVID Pneumonia. Within a minute, a nurse quickly unhooked Anita from the intravenous fluids they had just started, and they wheeled me outside into 95-degree heat while my wife walked slowly behind us. We were told not to worry about the wheelchair and left on the sidewalk to wait for our daughter's return. I was already having difficulty breathing, and the heat made it all the worse. We were astounded at the treatment, or lack thereof.

Although we didn't have a plan and had no idea how this would turn out, we just trusted that God was in control. *Do not let your hearts be troubled and do not be afraid.* (John 14:27 NIV)

At night, I attempted to fall asleep in different ways, but nothing seemed to work. Not being able to breathe was very unsettling. Most of us take for granted the ability to fill our lungs and live life. On one long, unbearable night of coughing and labored breathing, I left my bed and wrote out some thoughts I wanted to share with my kids in case I didn't get the chance to say it to them in person. Trust me, when you get to a place where you are writing letters like that to your family, your perspective on life has changed.

On the morning of September 2nd, my breathing was extremely labored, and my coughing was uncontrollable. Anita and I decided that I needed to go to the hospital. Since I was on a borrowed home oxygen machine and could not breathe without it, we had to determine whether my family could drive me the 25 minutes to the hospital or if we needed an ambulance. Anita had packed my bag, started the car to cool it down, and sat down to pray, asking the Lord for His clear direction. At that same moment, our daughter Karissa came into our bedroom to check on me and take my temperature. She quickly left the room and ran to Anita after seeing the results... 105.1. While Karissa packed my body with ice packs and cold compresses, Anita called the ambulance, which was quickly dispatched and arrived within five minutes.

> For the eyes of the Lord are on the righteous and His ears are attentive to their prayer. (1 Peter 3:12 NIV)

*And if we know that He hears us—whatever we ask—
we know that we have what we asked of Him. (1 John
5:15 NIV)*

I remember Anita and Karissa trying to stay composed as the ambulance arrived. I was strapped into the gurney and wheeled out to the ambulance. Everything happened so fast that I didn't have time to say goodbye. I'll never forget the feeling of seeing Anita standing there watching me get driven away.

Within a minute of arriving at the hospital, I was in the ER. I was put on 10 liters of oxygen, and although it was helping me, it was still difficult to breathe. I had absolutely no idea what to expect. I made some family calls, some of which were quite emotional. It is amazing how a near-death experience can bring a hard reality that you have one life to live, and you never know when it will end - for you or those around you.

After a few hours, I was transferred to a COVID-specific room and was only there for one day before the nurses told me I needed more oxygen than they could supply and was being transferred to the COVID Intensive Care Unit (ICU). Upon arriving, I immediately noticed that all of the rooms in the ICU had glass walls from floor to ceiling. I was brought to my room, where wires were connected to me so they could constantly monitor my vitals. There was definitely a different feel here - everything felt more purposeful. I was immediately put on 40 liters of pure oxygen.

During my first day in the ICU, I met both the head ICU doctor and the infectious disease (ID) doctor, and I had good conversations with each. The ID doctor asked if I had been vaccinated, and after hearing I had not been, he was clearly bothered. Soon afterward, he explained his response: his sister had chosen, for herself and her children, not to receive the COVID vaccine. Feeling that was an extremely unwise decision and not wanting unvaccinated people around him, he had officially cut her out of his life. I was shocked by this and quickly responded, telling him that family should supersede vaccination status and urging him to reconsider. After he left, I prayed that God would soften his heart.

I was happy that during his next visit, he apologized for how he had spoken during the previous day's discussion and said he was seriously considering reaching out to her. I encouraged him that he was making a great decision and, when he looks back on this season, he would appreciate changing his mind.

It's strange to say, but life became "normal" in the ICU. My "normal" day began with having my blood/gas checked daily at 4 am. A large needle would get stuck in my wrist, taking blood directly from the artery. Not fun, let me tell you. Normal blood/gas numbers are in the upper 80s, and mine had dropped to the low 40s. A few hours later, I would get a daily chest X-ray, the immediate image showing my almost completely white lungs, filled with fluid. Then, I was given a spirometer to check my lung capacity, resulting in a measuring indicator from 0 to 4,000. While an average healthy reading is above 1500, mine was barely reaching 100.

One night, just a couple of days into my time in the ICU, I was suddenly woken by several nurses who wanted me to sit up and take deep breaths (yeah, right). I asked them what was going on and was told my heart rate had dropped to 32!!!! They waited in my room until my heart rate increased, and as they walked out of the room, I remember asking them if I should just go back to sleep. It was surreal.

September 5th was our 29th wedding anniversary. I had now been in the ICU for three days, and things did not look good - everything on paper pointed toward my body failing. Anita and I would do video calls throughout each day, and I did the same with our kids. We had no choice since the hospital had implemented a strict no visitation policy. Anita had been doing tons of research on COVID and met several pivotal people as a result. It was recommended to her that I begin taking Ivermectin, so she contacted the lead ICU doctor, and he refused her request, saying it was hospital policy not to allow Ivermectin for any patients.

The more Anita researched, the more she learned how Ivermectin was proven to help specifically with COVID patients and how it seemed this life-saving medicine was purposefully getting shut down. All the while, I had Remdesivir running through my veins.

Throughout our lives, we have been told to "trust the experts." How could we ever question the people who had spent their lives dedicated to saving others and had vast knowledge in these matters?

My daily updates from the doctors were growing more serious each day. They wanted me to try a Bi-Pap machine to assist my breathing further. They brought the machine in and said, "Just strap this on, go to sleep, and you'll feel better in the morning." This turned out to be one of the more ridiculous things ever said to me. Using this device is equivalent to sticking your head out the window of a car going 150 miles per hour and then opening your mouth. There is a tube strapped directly to your face that forcefully shoots air into your mouth, which never stops. I stayed attached to this torture device for four hours and vowed to never put myself through that again. I had to pull it away from my face to try and take some small breaths that my body could handle before subjecting myself to another barrage of air.

I was in prayer throughout my stay and sang worship songs to pass the time - *Victory in Jesus; The Solid Rock; I'm Gonna See a Victory; Great Are You, Lord* - these songs repeated over and over in my mind throughout each day.

I felt the prayers of the literal thousands of people we had connected with throughout our years in ministry. *Because he has set his love upon Me, therefore I will deliver him; I will set him on high because he has known My name. He shall call upon Me, and I will answer him. I will be with him in trouble; I will deliver him and honor him.* (Psalm 91:14-15 NKJV)

Then, one day I felt God clearly saying, "I want you full time in ministry." My wife had served full-time for 24 years, and I had always given my free time, but now my full-time call was clear. I didn't hesitate. I knew that God wanted my full focus on Him, and it was time to make the decision to dedicate my life to full-time ministry. It was great to have that conversation with Anita, and we felt perfect peace, knowing I was following God's direction for my life. That was a conversation I will never forget.

A month prior, we had switched our general practitioner. We didn't know this at the time but it was definitely a God move. Anita received a call from our new GP to check in on our COVID recovery. When he asked how I was doing, she told him I was in the COVID ICU.

He was in shock. Anita explained that she tried talking to the ICU doctor to request Ivermectin and had been denied, so he asked for the doctor's name. After telling him, he informed Anita that he had previously worked with this doctor for 17 years and would give him a call. What are the chances that the doctor we just switched to a month earlier was a close work colleague of the head ICU doctor? God always has a plan. At that very moment, Anita, her parents, and our children went into prayer, calling down heaven to intervene. In the midst of that powerful prayer time, our GP called Anita back and said that he had personally pleaded with the ICU doctor to allow me Ivermectin, and he had acquiesced, allowing only one dose as long as my family would provide it.

> *And we know that in all things God works for the good of those who love Him, who have been called according to His purpose. (Romans 8:28 NIV)*

Anita immediately scrambled, asking her family and friends online if they had any spare Ivermectin, which was extremely difficult to get. A few hours later, Anita's sister got a response from someone from her church who had an extra dose. Karissa drove Anita to the next town around 9 pm to meet this angel woman, standing on the side of the road with the medication. They pulled up and rolled down the window; the lady said, "Are you Anita?" And the handoff was made!

Anita and Karissa raced to the hospital and met our other kids there. I told them I was on the first floor somewhere in the hospital, and the kids literally ran around the hospital until they found my room window. I cannot tell you how it felt to see them in real life after not seeing their faces for over a week. We did our best to hold back the tears, but they came anyway. They were instructed to leave the dose with the ER Security, and a few moments later, the nurse came in with the Ivermectin. That was at 11 pm. The next morning at 4 am, like clockwork, they took my daily blood/gas numbers, which shot up from 49 the previous morning to 93 - in just five hours. God is so good.

When Anita heard about the change in my condition, all personal restrictions were out the door. Her husband had to be saved, and she knew what it would take. A new friend and nurse spoke with Anita and recommended she "go rogue." Simply said, from that point forward, she did what she felt in her heart from God that she needed to do.

The next day, the physical therapist came into my room, first telling me how he was excited to meet me since he had heard about my quick turnaround and then asking if I wanted to try walking again. I hadn't stood in over a week, but I was excited at the opportunity. I could barely stand up, so I held onto the portable air machine for support. I slowly walked a lap around the ICU unit and saw room after room with people hooked up to ventilators, not moving. After one lap around, I stuck to the hallway where I wouldn't see the other patients. It was too much.

Things happened very quickly after that. I received the news that I was leaving the ICU! As they wheeled me out, I thanked all the nurses and said, "You must live for this moment - when you get someone out of the ICU!"

They responded, "Ron, you are the only one that has made it out of the ICU. Everyone around you is dying."

That was one of the most sobering moments of my life. I couldn't respond as the immenseness of that statement hit me. I was so grateful for all the prayers from people around the world, the tenacious spirit of my wife, who never gave up on me, and MOST IMPORTANT of all, for our Heavenly Father, who orchestrated my healing.

Looking back, I am amazed at the peace God provided me. I have heard story after story from other people that went through major mental anguish during their COVID ICU stays, and I am so happy that wasn't my experience. When you put your trust and faith in the Almighty, nothing is impossible. My story is evidence.

Since God saved my life, we have been on a whirlwind tour. I have learned the enormous opportunity God gives us with every breath, and I intend to use each breath for His glory. We met General Flynn and the *Iowa Momma Bears*. We spent an evening with Bo Snerdley and was interviewed for his COVID focused podcast. We started *Frontline Community Care Network*, a group of doctors, nurses, health experts, and tenacious nonmedical folks like us who are proactively providing education and services to assist our communities in wellness. We also started *Spark New Life* to help coach and mentor people financially and in life to bring balance and freedom. Your life is a gift from God. Are you using the power God gives you through His Spirit and each breath in your lungs to be a light in your family? Your community? Are you using your precious days to reach others with the saving knowledge of Jesus Christ? It's never too late to make a change in your life or the life of someone around you – your words can have eternal implications for others. I invite you to join me and create your own legacy. Don't waste a single breath.

My life verse: *But in your hearts revere Christ the Lord. Always be prepared to give an answer to everyone who asks you to give a reason for the hope that you have. But do this with gentleness and respect.* (1 Peter 3:15 NIV)

FAITH TO OVERCOME DISEASE

When we are infected or affected by an illness, we can choose how we view that disease. Everybody, sooner or later, gets sick. Nobody doubts this. A disease can rise quickly, seemingly from nowhere, making us wonder where it came from. While Scripture gives us examples of why some people become sick, the reason for our sickness is not always understood. And even if it was, no disease is easy to withstand. Yet, with God's grace, we can persevere amid disease if we hold steadfastly to our faith and the peace God provides.

Throughout the Bible, we see examples of individuals inflicted with terrible diseases. We can ask ourselves why. Why did they suffer, and why do we have to suffer? Why do the ones we love have to suffer? It is interesting that often there is a purpose for the afflictions of those in the Bible and that God deemed their circumstances valuable enough to share in His Word.

Let's take a look at Job. Although Job was blameless, upright, and feared God, God used Job's traumas to draw him closer to Himself. (You can read about this in the book of Job, chapters one and two.) One reason the Lord allows evil and suffering is because He can bring good from it.

Then there is Naaman. When Naaman, the commander of the Syrian Army, got a terrible infectious disease, he turned to God the Creator to heal him. He humbled himself and, in faith, turned to God—and God healed him! (2 Kings 5:15)

Many other people in the Bible were afflicted with terrible diseases that God used to turn their attention to Him.

God wants you to know that no matter what you may be walking through and despite whatever plagues your body or soul, having strong faith and trusting in God's plan can position you for a testimony to the world and bring you lasting peace.

If you knew the almighty God wanted to use you to show His miraculous power through your battles of sickness, would you be willing to walk through the fire to be a vessel for Him? It's something to think about and ask yourself. Even if a disease took your life, would you be ok with God using you this way? These are difficult questions, but with courage, we can say yes to God. It takes powerful courage to trust an illness into God's care and leave it in His hands. Only He can give you the strength to endure and the will to continue.

There is so much to learn while enduring an illness. Through suffering, we learn to have compassion for others. Through disease, we can learn to help and depend on each other. Tumultuous times that test our faith and love can make our faith and love grow stronger. Through pain, we learn to turn our lives over to God and gain wisdom from Him about what we can control and what we cannot. Surrendering to God everything that is out of our control, including disease, releases us to grow spiritually as we depend on Him through challenging times.

Only God can give you the strength to endure and the will to continue. Remember, God says, *"I am the Lord, who heals you."* (Exodus 15:26 NIV) Pray and surrender any disease to God and ask Him for the courage needed to seek and find His will through your disease.

Oh Lord, by these things men live, and in all these is the life of my spirit; restore me to health and let me live! (Isaiah 38:16 AMP)

. . . .

DOUG SAHM

Doug Sahm was born on December 13, 1977, outside Los Angeles, California. From birth until now, the word home has represented many feelings, locations, people, and occurrences for him. Many changes have been hard to accept, but now, through GOD'S guidance, the result is love.

Doug has an amazing wife named Sara Sahm, who is a best-selling author with Women World Leaders. Doug and Sara have two spectacular daughters named Ember and River. As a family, they all look to God for direction and faith. Doug and his brothers do business in industrial real estate, and they extrude and anodize aluminum products. Art is one of the abilities that GOD has given Doug. He is a talented artist who loves to use color to express emotion. You can check out his work at dougsahmart.com. Doug also loves golf, working out, the beach, church, friends, and helping other people.

LETTING GOD'S LOVE BREAK OUR CHAINS

BY DOUG SAHM

I am a true believer, and I'd like to share some challenging pieces of my past, hoping to show what GOD can do for us. As I grew up, the word GOD was viewed and used with demands that created a form of spiritual control and guilt. My first reaction was fear, my second reaction was anger, and after that, I felt I had to run from structured religion. Outside control was my enemy, and I felt rules were there to be challenged. I ignored my relationship with GOD and took over my spiritual steering, which guided me down rough roads through many crashes and close encounters with death. I called those things "my life." My selfishness took over, and love was blocked, so my eyes could not see it, but my injured heart felt the pain that was created. From my decisions, pain and a lost soul were born. As you read through my struggles, view them as the pathways GOD used to show me the way back into His arms with mercy. "Wow!" is what I feel when I look at all GOD provides and how foolish it was when I ran away from His love. Countless quotes in the Bible show me that GOD wants to give us love and direction; I will share some of them with you. *In all your ways acknowledge him, and he will make straight your paths.* (Proverbs 3:6 ESV)

I am a believer, but that has not always directed how I've lived my life. Thankfully, through spiritual healing, grace, love, and guidance from GOD, it now is. When I look at my life, I can see countless blessings I missed because I lacked the belief required. Life has shown me that when it is "a mess," some spiritual chains must be broken so healing can take place. It has taken a long time to realize that the only way chains become gifts is through GOD's guidance, not man's desires. When I run my life based on selfish intentions, I begin to lose dreams, friends, family, love, guidance, safety, and hope. That shows me that faith is not just a word, it is a Savior, and GOD is its creator.

There are three painful emotional chains that I want to share with you. Then at the end, I have three simple questions for you to ask yourself. These three chains all represent different kinds of pain. One is from me to myself, one is from someone else to me, and the final one is from someone else to themself. Here is a quote to start your journey through my chains and GOD's ability to guide people home. *But the path of the righteous is like the light of dawn, which shines brighter and brighter until full day.* (Proverbs 4:18 ESV)

The first painful chain I want to share is addiction and how it took over my life. Many different addictions, including drugs, alcohol, women, money, and emotional dominance, have run my life. Without GOD, they all can easily take over, and that usually starts with ego. My addictions have all damaged my mind, body, and spirit in a slow, deep, and painful way. When addiction runs my life, the only thing I know how to do is use more until my feelings are lost or forgotten. With my feelings blinded by addiction, GOD was not where I saw "my way out." I often asked the dreadful question, "Is there a way out?"

Addiction runs deep on both sides of my family. For me, a solution felt close to impossible. When I look at my past, I see that my addiction destroyed people, relationships, businesses, finances, and opportunities. That destruction kept showing up with no concern for the mess it was creating. The damages addictions caused were horrible. All other people could see was addiction destroying my life. They created emotional and drug-based separation from myself and GOD. These separations started with other people and quickly became a separation from who GOD wants me to be. As I fell deeper, the whirlwind of negativity pulled me away from any chance of feeling joy. All it delivered was pain. With addictions digging deeper into my soul, my visions of life became very narrow and heartless. If you are an addict, whatever you are addicted to becomes the leader of your life and the enemy of stability. Countless attempts to become sober on my own or from different rehabs never did enough to keep me clean. That is part of my truth because I was not allowing GOD to lead my future.

My life stayed like that for over twenty years. Until one day, I was on my knees begging GOD to show me the way out, take control of my life, and guide my future. Living with GOD's guidance and on the path that He provides has given me a real form of clarity and serenity. With GOD in my life, I know addiction is not there for me to be a victim of.

GOD's path is full of grace, and it helps me through sorrow. If I start feeling comfortable, my ego looks for control. If I do things my way or tell myself, "Don't worry, GOD won't mind," failure is always on its way. In my life, many reoccurring thoughts, actions, judgments, and beliefs pushed me away from the love of GOD. Today I can see, feel, process, react clearly, and live with the strength of GOD's love.

To get out of my addiction, I had to admit failure, let go of my plans and accept the guidance from faith that GOD provides. Easy is the last word I would use to describe letting go of having control, but it is the first thing I would use to describe letting in GOD's love and forgiveness. Addiction has always been part of my life, but with GOD, I am sober today.

Fear and anger used to be the initial feelings I felt when the topic of addiction became part of a conversation. Now, thanks to GOD's gift of sobriety, I can help others understand what addiction is. Understanding the truth about my addictions is ongoing, and I let GOD lead that. My painful addictions have become a gift through spiritual sobriety, helping others find GOD, and showing others how to get sober through faith. "Wow!" is the first reaction that comes to my mind when I look at this chapter of my life, and "Thank you!" is my first outgoing prayer that I send to GOD. Things like this show me that bits of heaven are here for us if we allow ourselves to accept them. This Bible quote reminds me of how open GOD's arms are for us when we believe, *But those who hope in the LORD will renew their strength. They will soar on wings like eagles; they will run and not grow weary; they will walk and not be faint.* (Isaiah 40:31 NIV)

The second painful chain in my life that I want to share with you is drug dealing gone astray. At 18, I was living in northern California, getting ready to start attending the Academy of Arts College in San Francisco. Life offered me the opportunity to seek one of my dreams—to study art. GOD was showing me a true glance of a gift He provided for me, but I was too blind to see it. At that time, my life felt stable, and addiction was not directing me. At least, that was what I believed. Money was starting to become something I felt was not only a desire but also a necessity. The place I worked only paid me a small portion of what I believed was required. The first thing that came to my mind to make more money the easy way was to deal cocaine.

Naivety was my go-to excuse for my stupid actions. Greed and selfish actions blinded me from my relationship with GOD until it became forgotten. Being a dealer started as an easy way to make quick cash with very little time or labor. It all began with a partnership between myself and someone who I believed was a close friend. Quickly I started to see that there was no friendship—only lies, manipulation, greed, violence, and distrust. My naivety sure did a good job blocking my vision of what was going on.

Then one day at my studio, I had to go to work, but my partner said, "Can I please use the bathroom?"

My response was, "Go ahead, but hurry up because I cannot be late."

Then he went into my bathroom, and when he walked out, he shot me point blank. That shot went between my eyes, and he left me for dead. I separated from my body, then I saw myself and screamed, "Please, GOD, I am not ready to go."

In my life, betrayal was something I knew about, but it was never something that had become part of my life. At that moment, I saw a bright flash; I reentered my body and called 911. GOD gave me another chance through a blessing that only He could deliver. My studio was close to Stanford University Medical Center, where I was taken. The doctors put me into an induced coma that lasted more than a month. Part of my forehead was removed to release pressure on my brain, and several tubes were attached to my body to feed me and take care of my other health needs. While in a coma, I was flown to Scripps Hospital in Encinitas, California, where I was cared for until one of GOD's blessings led me out of the coma. "Thank you, GOD!" is what my emotions feed me when I think about those moments of my past.

After, some of the first things said about me were, "He may never walk, talk, and or ever be able to live on his own again."

Those words were painful and scared me because I had no idea what my future would be. But GOD had other plans for me, and through several medical centers, physical rehabs, brain specialty centers, and the love that surrounded me, I was able to recover. None of this would have been possible without GOD's grace.

Since this happened, I have been able to help others in countless ways due to the wisdom and experience I gained, and I know that this is how I can give thanks to GOD. The Bible reminds me of this repeatedly, and this quote matches what I feel over and over again. *I will give thanks to you, Lord, with all of my heart; I will tell of all your wonderful deeds.* (Psalm 9:1 NIV)

The third painful chain I am sharing with you is based on security and a quick feeling of loss. I hope that this piece of my past can show you how GOD can become our never-ending path to security. Unfortunately, this piece of my truth is still painful because of how deep it digs into my emotional basis, but I also use that pain to create stability. My story starts with a brief explanation of my childhood.

When I was five, my parents divorced due to drug addiction, adultery, emotional pain, money, and lack of GOD in their relationship. After they divorced, my dad went his own way, and I lived with my mom. I no longer had a relationship with my dad due to the emotional separation and physical gap. My relationship with my mom was what I relied upon to show me how to grow up and live. Life was hard for us, and at times, things looked weary, but that only made our relationship stronger. Throughout my childhood, my mom was my guide, my teacher, and my hero. During that part of my life, I never understood what it felt like to have a male role model. That absence created a deep hole in my heart that I would not be able to fill until my relationship with GOD became my anchor.

My relationship with my mom started changing as I got older. As I entered my teenage years, my life became a whirlwind full of poor decisions, drugs, greed, women, rebellion, and no relationship with GOD. During that time, my relationship with my mom became shallow, and interactions with my dad were close to nonexistent. When I was 15, sobriety finally became part of my dad's life, and rehab was starting to become part of mine. After he became sober, my dad's demands became all that mattered to him. For me, living under his terms was emotionally draining, but it was required to have a relationship with him. When I look back at this, I'm reminded that honesty was the only thing my mom required. But with GOD's help, I have accepted the type of relationship my dad offers, no longer expecting the relationship I have been seeking since childhood.

Now that I have shared a little bit of the basis of this chain in my life, I will share its actions. My mom's battles with men, drugs, alcohol, family, success, emotions, and GOD created an internal war between her mind, body, and soul. This war was nothing but sneaky and destructive. It created severe fluctuations in her physical health, her ability to communicate, and her self-worth, leaving her empty inside. My mom often showed her pain with a bright smile and empty eyes.

Unfortunately, my life, addictions, and lack of a relationship with GOD created a distance that fell between my mom and me. Yet, when I share things about my mom and our past, I see that despite the separation, we were always there for each other. My mom's addictions and lack of self-worth are what ended her life through suicide. My immediate response was, "Why did you do this?" and "Why didn't you ask me for help?" Quickly after those responses, all my emotions surfaced, and I became emotionally lost. I fell to my knees and asked GOD for some help and guidance. Since my mom's suicide, GOD has helped me find strength and encouragement from my painful loss. Through prayer and direction, my broken security has been renewed. GOD's guidance becomes brighter every day, and I know that my mom is safe with Him in heaven. The Bible offers me comfort, and I pray that this quote offers comfort to everyone who lives life broken. *The LORD is close to the brokenhearted and saves those who are crushed in spirit.* (Psalm 34:18, NIV)

I hope that these painful chains that GOD turned into spiritual growths can help you see what GOD has to offer. Here are some truths that GOD has given me to keep our relationship healthy. What amazes me is that they come from my three painful chains.

- When I look at the chain of addiction and my separation from the destruction, I clearly see a piece of GOD's grace.

- When I look at the chain of betrayal, I am now able to see GOD's ability to redirect us through devotion.

- My painful chain of abandonment has shown me that GOD can turn separation into faith.

These feelings and reactions are only possible because of how much GOD loves us. In my life, there are countless blessings that GOD has offered me, and I can see that pain in my life has blocked me from this truth. Because of everything I have been through, I know that only GOD is why I am still alive and able to share these stories with you.

As I come to the end of these three chains, I have three questions for you:

- Do you live in emotional or physical pain?

- Do you ask for help when you need it?

- Is GOD who you turn to for guidance?

These questions may seem easy to answer but telling the full truth is always hard to do.

Here are three quotes from the Bible that remind me GOD is always there to help us through.

> *If we confess our sins, he is faithful and just to forgive us our sins and purify us from all unrighteousness. (1 John 1:9 NIV)*

> *Be kind and compassionate to one another, forgiving each other, just as Christ God forgave you. (Ephesians 4:32 NIV)*

> *The Lord your God goes with you; he will never leave you nor forsake you. (Deuteronomy 31:6 NIV)*

This was not my entire story, it was only a piece, but I wanted to share with you how GOD, in His love, broke my chains. I know things would not be what they are if I had denied His love. And I know accepting and living in His love will break your chains, too.

.

GEORGE MATTHEW MCNALLY

George Matthew McNally—entrepreneur, businessman, fisherman, and recovering alcoholic—grew up in South Florida and was raised in a Catholic home. George was introduced to Jesus at a very young age. The scripture Proverbs 22:6 tells the story of George's path through life.

Train up a child in the way he should go, and when he is old he will not depart from it. (Proverbs 22:6 NKJV)

From alcohol and drug addiction to a 90-mile-per-hour motorcycle crash, his life came full circle when he finally quit running from God and realized he needed help. Jesus was faithful and came through in a big way.

Successful in business, one of George's greatest achievements so far was when he was called to the addiction industry and took ownership of *House of Principles Recovery Residence.* In partnership with God, "HOP" helped thousands of men find Christ, with recovery, family, careers, and so many other blessings that often come when we trade hurt for hope and a new way of life.

RUN FROM COPS...
BUT NOT FROM GOD

BY GEORGE MATTHEW MCNALLY

From as far back As I can remember, there was always talk of God in and around the McNally family. "God d**n it" was a very common term. "Oh my God," usually came in a close second. All kidding aside, God was always there; I just wasn't mature enough to pick up on it back then. It took one heck of a ride, literally, for the "Big Guy" to finally get my attention. I had to go through what I now know as God's refining fire, a 15-year gauntlet of different adventures, some good and some bad. Those fifteen years were a testament to the fact that I'm a selfish human being with an oversized ego and the same size inferiority complex. I needed to find my place. I needed to find my people. I needed to grow up.

Mom and Dad came to Florida in 1966 with two small kids and no money. I can assure you that was not Mom's plan; because she told me many times. My father had a big 90-acre property in the woods of East Durham, New York, close to the Catskill mountains - a summer getaway for the locals who didn't want to go too far. The bar/nightclub was one building, and the bungalow was the "hotel" where guests could rent rooms to stay for the weekend. Mom was looking forward to raising a couple of kids and caring for a husband who had money. She was looking forward to being a homemaker. She said it felt like a kick in the gut when my father had his first heart attack. He was only 48, and she was 33. I was 2 ½ years old, and my brother Brian was an infant. It wasn't how she envisioned her life playing out. Well, "playing out" might not be the best way to put it.

Mom, Jean Kathryn Fust McNally, was born on July 24, 1933, to George and Margaret Fust. I never met my grandfather, but I know I would have loved him. My Nana was a different story. Nana was a hard German woman who survived the depression and didn't know how to show feelings. Mom, an only child, had a tough childhood and unfortunately didn't quite get the emotional support she needed, which affected her later in life. From her upbringing, however, she developed a good work ethic, and when my dad got sick, she knew what she had to do. And that she did. She waited tables and went to school at the same time, all while dealing with a family with kids. She got a degree in the insurance industry and opened an Allstate agency in Boynton Beach, Florida, to finish her career. She was an incredible example. If only I had listened to her.

I don't know about you, but I am one of those people who always have to learn things the hard way. I was a typical kid. I just wanted to fit in, just wanted to be accepted. I always felt like something was missing, which all changed when I found drugs, alcohol, and fast motorcycles. By the time I entered my freshman year in high school, I had already experienced what drugs and alcohol could do for me, and I loved it. It quickly became part of my life. I always hung out with the older crowd so I could drink and party with them. I don't think I had yet crossed that line into full-blown addiction, but I was well on my way. I still managed to get decent grades in school up to this point. My freshman year was a big turning point for me as it was my first experience with public school. John I. Leonard High School was right down the street from our house, and Dad, being the frugal one, talked Mom into letting us give it a try. Since I had already gravitated to the "bad element," I was off to the races. Fifteen years old, and I thought I knew it all. I started skipping school, smoking pot every day, and hanging out with kids who stole things from stores and broke into cars and houses. Back then, we had split sessions, which meant that juniors and seniors went to class in the morning, and freshmen and sophomores started at noon. Perfect! I would collect five dollars from a customer on my paper route every morning and would buy six joints of marijuana for that five dollars so I could get high with my friends.

Life was grand, or so I thought. Then one night, we were out in the neighborhood when my buddy "Pete" picked up a rock and threw it through a window of a house belonging to one of the girls we went to school with. Then, he yelled, calling the girl a derogatory name as we all took off on our bicycles, adrenaline flowing. About an hour later, we were at Cumberland Farms when the clerk called the police because she thought we were being "dangerous" on our bikes in the parking lot. Two cops showed up and one left. The next thing I heard was my name coming through the police radio. They put us in the back of separate cars and took us right back to the house with the broken window. We were done!

For 2 ½ weeks, Pete chased me around school, saying I ratted on him to the police. He told everyone he was going to beat me up, and that's exactly what he did. One day, he dragged me off my bicycle, sat on my chest, and proceeded to bloody my face. Up until then, I had never been in a real fight. But this was high school, not like the little grade school playground scuffles we got in over a kickball game. I can still hear my mom, "Jesus says we turn the other cheek." Yeah right! I wasn't feeling much like Jesus. I wanted to beat him to a pulp, but I didn't know how. Well, Dad wasn't too happy about my bloody nose or Mom's Jesus comment. He vowed that this would never happen again, and within the next few weeks, I was enrolled in the Martial Arts Academy in West Palm Beach. Grand Master Warren Siciliano taught in this dojo, it was called Karado Karate. I fell in love! This was a big thing for me. As much as this could have been a major turning point in my life, I was still running the show. And when I run the show, the show doesn't come off too well!

Money was always tight, so Mom and Dad scrimped and saved wherever they could. The motorcycle driving age was 15, so my dad, "Mr. Frugal," decided that Brian and I should ride motorbikes to school. He found a great deal on matching CB 125 Honda motorcycles. Mine was blue; I hated it and vowed to upgrade it as soon as possible. So, I worked construction during the summer and at Home Depot after my senior year and bought a 1983 Yamaha Seca 900 sport bike. It was candy apple red with black and gray stripes and graphics. It was new and FAST! I loved it.

I never had a problem drawing attention to myself. I learned at a young age that negative attention was better than no attention, so I acted out often. And I used my new bike to help - doing stoppies, burnouts, donuts, or whatever request was presented. Wheelies were my favorite, and I was often seen standing on the back pegs at 80 miles an hour on I-95 as I kept up with traffic on one wheel. This was totally insane, but I was good at it and loved how it made me feel. One night, a cop saw me leaving Lake Worth Beach on the back wheel, and I saw him reach for his radio as we turned the corner. We crossed a bridge, and then there was another cop with the blue lights on. We all took off, and I got away, but that was the beginning of the end for me.

Talk about adrenaline! Wow! I loved it! That was better going 145 mph on the highway. The thrill of victory! And I thought to myself, *They'll NEVER catch me.* So from then on, I ran. I ran from every cop who chased me, from State Troopers to local police. I got away 30 to 40 times. But then came that one fateful night that changed my life forever. That time, I didn't get away.

I always told myself never to run on A1A because it runs along the beach, and the only way on or off the island is the closest bridge. It was November 24, 1984, around 6:30 PM, and there was a tropical depression beating up the area. Wind and rain pelted me as I rode my Seca 900 heading northbound from Boynton Inlet. A car passed me going south. I said to myself, "Wow, I hope that wasn't a cop," even though I didn't think I was speeding. When I turned to look, sure enough, there were red and blue lights, and he was turning around.

I took off without even thinking. It was almost instinctive. I was flying! Up ahead, I saw more red and blue lights. The road was blocked.

I thought to myself, *You're in trouble now.* I had never been in this situation before. I was scared, but I knew I couldn't stop. So I went around the roadblock, through the grass, and when I got to the light at Lantana Beach, I made a left turn to head west over the bridge. I rolled on the throttle, the 900cc motor screamed and I flew over the bridge like a bullet fired from a gun. With six or seven marked police cruisers with lights and sirens blaring right on my tail, I said to myself, "I gotta turn, I gotta turn, I gotta turn!" All of a sudden, there was a hill...wait...I'm not familiar....BAMM!

Right after the hill, the road dipped off to the left. I was running at about 70 to 80 miles an hour when I crested the hill, and I couldn't make the turn. I hit the back of the wooden fence that surrounded the yard on the corner, and I went through it. I took out a grapefruit tree and hit the side of the house, leaving a tire mark on the yellow paint. Another few feet to the north, I would have hit the back of the house and been dead instantly. I landed in the front yard, but the bike kept tumbling and landed in the driveway across the street. I knew I was hurt badly. I was in and out of consciousness. Witnesses said that I tried to get up and run. I lost almost eight pints of blood on the scene and was told that I coded (died) at the emergency room twice that night. Wow! I didn't realize it then, but I sure do know it now; only by the grace of a loving God did I make it through such a horrific crash.

I spent the next three months and three weeks in the hospital. When I hit the fence, trees, and house, I suffered "crush syndrome" on the left side of my body. I broke my left wrist, elbow, shoulder, knee cap, femur, right arm, and right leg. My left arm and leg were so badly smashed that the doctors wrote in my chart that amputation was a good possibility. About one week after the crash, I was diagnosed with

UNITED MEN OF HONOR:
OVERCOMING ADVERSITY THROUGH FAITH

renal failure. The doctors discovered my kidneys had also shut down from the shock and trauma to my body

My poor parents. November 24, 1984, was way before cell phones. The house phone rang at about 10:30 PM that Sunday night, and Mom let the answering machine pick up as she sat and watched TV. "This is nurse so-and-so from JFK hospital. Your son was involved in a bad motorcycle crash..." That was a message no parent ever wanted to get. Mom said she had a hard time getting dressed to make that 15-minute drive to the hospital. Ironically, we were all too familiar with that hospital. I had worked on a construction crew there for two summers, and my father had just spent three weeks there earlier that year due to a heart attack. I think that was his sixth or seventh. I can't even begin to imagine what my parents went through those following few nights and weeks. Mom was always my biggest fan. I was like her in many ways; we used to joke, saying I was her carbon copy with different plumbing.

Mom was my role model, my confidant, and my friend. Only I didn't realize it until I matured. Mom taught us about God and His Son Jesus, and we went to church every Sunday. She enrolled me in a Catholic school in kindergarten, which began my eight-year journey dealing with priests and nuns. I hated it. I didn't understand it then, but everything I learned played a part in building the man I have become, and I'm grateful for that.

So there I was, laid up in a hospital bed with two broken arms, two broken legs, and all kinds of other injuries. I told you in the beginning that it took a lot to get my attention. I was a big strong kid who lifted weights, practiced karate, and had a career ahead as a pro fighter - if I had wanted it. But one bad decision threw all that in the toilet. Still, the fact that I was in great shape made a big difference in my survival.

After 30+ surgical procedures and dialysis three times a week for six weeks, my health stabilized. My kidneys started functioning properly, amazing the doctors. I was grateful, and so was everyone else. When I was finally able to get out of bed after enduring everything from external fixation to wearing a body cast for six weeks, my eyes caught my reflection in the mirror. I stood there for about 10 seconds before it hit me. *Look at what you've done!* I lost it and started to cry. Humility tried to creep in, but I wouldn't let it. My poor body was all busted up. The full-length cast on my left leg had hinges so I could bend my knee. I looked at it and thought, *No more kickboxing for me, I guess.* But then I caught myself, and my ego took over again. *I know what to do. I'll survive. I'll figure it out.*

And so it began.

I've always been a salesman, per se, so I returned to that "trade" for almost ten years after my crash. Knowing I had to survive, I became one of the county's most prominent small-time dope dealers. I carried large quantities of illegal substances into the local clubs and hot spots in town. There were several times I got very lucky and avoided situations that could have put me in prison for a long time. Right before Thanksgiving 1992, just after Hurricane Andrew made landfall in Miami, I was living with my girlfriend in her townhouse. We were both working in the little Mexican restaurant that she was in the process of buying. Things were good until they weren't. We were both drinking and smoking lots of weed, and I was taking Percocet like candy. The economy was not good, and we struggled to make it after the storm hit. The house was in foreclosure, the restaurant payments were in arrears, and one morning when we woke up to go to work, the car was gone – having been repossessed. There was no place to go but home to Mom.

Mom was living by herself and had been alone since Dad passed away from his 9th heart attack in 1986. Mom told me I could stay with her temporarily, but I had to go to rehab if I wanted to live there. I agreed but asked for her consideration to put it off for a bit since it was almost Thanksgiving and Christmas was right around the corner, followed by my birthday on December 29. "I can't go now," I said. "Can I wait until after January 1?" She didn't like it but agreed.

A few days after New Year's 1993, Mom reminded me of our deal. I thought quickly and, half joking and half serious, said, "Mom, the Super Bowl is only three weeks away..."

She wasn't amused in the least. So, on February 9, 1993, I entered a treatment center and have not had a drink of alcohol since.

In treatment, I had a very powerful spiritual experience that opened my heart to the Lord. I saw a picture of a human heart with a door on it. Jesus was knocking on the door. When I looked closely, there was no handle on the door; it could only be opened from the inside. I opened the door to my heart that day, and what a ride it has been.

Who knows where I would have ended up without my mom. One Bible verse that means the world to me is Proverbs 22:6. *Train up a child in the way he should go, And when he is old he will not depart from it.* (NKJV) This is 100% true for me. Mom and Dad tried to teach, lead and guide us, but my way had to be defined by me. It's now been almost 30 years since I went to that treatment center, and I couldn't ask for a better life. Yes, life has its ups and downs. But if I had written down what I imagined success would be for me as I began my path to sobriety, I would have sold myself unbelievably short.

I stumbled into a career in the car business, and when that ride ended, Mom helped me purchase a business in the recovery field allowing us to help people and give back. That business was called *House Of Principles Recovery Residence For Men.* I am blessed and grateful that God chose me to be the steward of that business and gave me a front-row seat to miracles that happened before my eyes. I was humbled to be a witness to hundreds if not thousands of guys finding God, recovery, family, and career—all as a result of surrendering to a new way of life. They say humble pie doesn't taste good, but it sure is good for you. I'm glad I have had a few spoonfuls over the years. I needed them.

My life is much different now than it used to be. Today, I know that I am just a speck of sand on the beach of life and that God is in control. He had His hand on me throughout my life, and despite the difficult paths I chose, He never gave up on me. We can run from our responsibilities, our past, and even from the cops. But we can never run from God.

I cried,
And You heard my voice.
For You cast me into the deep,
Into the heart of the seas,
And the floods surrounded me;
All Your billows and Your waves passed over me.
Then I said, 'I have been cast out of Your sight;
Yet I will look again toward Your holy temple.'
The waters surrounded me, even to my soul;
The deep closed around me;
Weeds were wrapped around my head.
I went down to the moorings of the mountains;
The earth with its bars closed behind me forever;
Yet You have brought up my life from the pit,
O Lord, my God.
(Jonah 2:2-6 NKJV)

FAITH TO OVERCOME ADDICTIONS

Our ability to enjoy life the way God designed us is due to the goodness of God. Therefore, we cannot take our eyes off Him if we wish to maintain a fully satisfied life.

Addiction is a disease of self-destructive behavior that pulls us away from the fulfillment only God can offer. Becoming addicted can stem from a lack of satisfaction in life because we feel that a needed component is missing for our completion. The addict looks for comfort from the world instead of from God. They seek a vice to help them deal with stress, escape, or situations beyond their control.

Addictions cause the addict to think they need something to satisfy them, leading them to wander as they seek ways to meet their increased temptations and desires down a path of desperation and despair. Before long, they realize all complete satisfaction is gone. The entangled web of destruction caused by addictive behaviors grows as their eyes are fixed on themselves, not God.

The world is full of trials and temptations that can potentially become addictions. This long list includes drugs, alcohol, and lustful pursuits. Yielding to destructive behavior brings misery. The moment we grasp our desire, we may feel good or even great, but the longing is never truly fulfilled, and the pain and struggles return, often bringing a feeling like the end of the world is upon us. Then, we repeatedly give in to the temptation as we sink deeper into the pit of despair.

It is vital to know that love, forgiveness, and redemption are core values, and no matter which path you followed in the past or are on now, there is hope for you to release any addiction in the name of Jesus.

The Bible clearly talks about self-discipline and how important it is to focus and stay on the right path.

No temptation has overtaken you except what is common to mankind. And God is faithful; he will not let you be tempted beyond what you can bear. But when you are tempted, he will also provide a way out so that you can endure it. (1 Corinthians 10:13 NIV)

Submit your addiction to God. Be prayerful and heartfelt with the surrender of your addiction, and you can be assured that God will step in. When you allow Him the ability to take over what you can no longer control, He intervenes. It is important to immerse yourself in God's word and communicate with Him continuously. That which has a stronghold over you should not be fought without the power of the Living God.

The Lord is my rock and my fortress and my deliverer; my God is my rock, in whom I take refuge, my shield and the horn of my salvation, my stronghold. (Psalm 18:2 NIV)

Get yourself out of harm's way and stop self-medicating. Surrender your heart to God. Arm yourself with God's provisions. Put on the whole armor of God so you can combat the addictions that you struggle with. (Ephesians 6:10-17) Find a Band of Brothers who will hold you accountable. And stay away from those doing what you are so desperately trying to quit.

Do not be misled: Bad company corrupts good character. (1 Corinthians 15:33 NIV)

. . . .

JOSE CHEO RODRIGUEZ

 Jose "Cheo" Rodriguez, born and raised in Puerto Rico, graduated from King's College in Pennsylvania with a bachelor's in Business Management. Additionally, he received a Diploma in Risk Management & Insurance from The College of Insurance, currently known as St. John's University in New York. Jose has worked at Fortune 500 companies and was part owner and General Manager of Shred-It Puerto Rico.

In 2002, Cheo married Ginny Rodriguez. Together, they have two wonderful kids, Alanis and Gian. In 2014, they moved to South Florida, where Cheo and Ginny both experienced life changes that led them to accept Jesus as their Lord and Savior. They have since dedicated their lives to representing and bringing Jesus to everything they do.

Jose "Cheo" Rodriguez is the President of Handyman PRO Solutions, Vice President of Heavenly Hands Property Services, and a Board Member of Heavenly Hands Foundation. Ginny and Cheo joined forces with Heavenly Hands Property Services and now have a team of 60+ and several vertical companies under the Heavenly Hands Foundation that point to the true owner of everything, GOD.

GOD SPEAKS IN MYSTERIOUS WAYS; ALWAYS BE READY TO LISTEN

BY JOSE CHEO RODRIGUEZ

2012 was one of the darkest years in my life. I had no identity and felt so empty inside. I was trying to fill that emptiness with anything and everything I could find. I was a man of the world, and even though I knew of God, I had no real relationship with Him. I was a non-practicing Catholic, having been raised in the Catholic religion. But I knew something or someone was missing in my life.

Do you know those vision boards where you fill out the four quadrants - one for personal, one for business, one for financial, and one for spiritual? I had no problem filling out three quadrants but could not complete the fourth. I bet you can guess which one. I thought I had a relationship with God my way.

At this time, I had been married to my beautiful, patient, and very forgiving wife for ten years but had not let go of my old ways. Following my emptiness, I started looking for the wrong people to fill the gaps in my life, and sadly, I found them in other women. My decisions took a toll on our relationship to the point where my wife and I decided to separate and stop living together. I was so irresponsible back then that instead of leaving our home, I forced Ginny to rent an apartment while I stayed in the house. We shared the two kids as if we were divorced, having them stay with me for a week and with her for the next week. I was living a wild life and was completely unfaithful to her any chance I got. It was as if I was in my college years, living carefree with no regard for any responsibility or concern for whose lives I was affecting. I did not respect myself or anyone else at this point.

> Do you not know that the unrighteous will not inherit the kingdom of God? Do not be deceived. Neither fornicators, nor idolaters, nor adulterers, nor homosexuals, nor sodomites, nor revilers, nor extortioners will inherit the kingdom of God. And such were some of you. But you were washed, but you were sanctified, but you were justified in the name of the Lord Jesus and by the Spirit of our God. (1 Corinthians 6:9-11 NKJV)

A year went by, and there was no resolution between my wife and me. I was so lost that I had a lover, and a lover from the lover. Finally, my wife got fed up and, not seeing any easy way out of this situation, asked me for a divorce. I happily agreed, very eager to get my marriage over with so I could be "FREE" and "HAPPY." Little did I know what was about to happen.

My wife coordinated everything for the divorce, including getting the lawyer and setting the final appointment. But something inside me did not feel right. So, I looked for confirmation that what I was about to do was correct. In seeking confirmation, I decided to stop by a fortune teller and get a consultation on my way to the lawyer's office for our divorce appointment. As I walked in, the lady looked at me and immediately and without hesitation said, and I quote, because I will never forget those words, "The one you want to leave is the one that God has for you, and the one you want to be with has the devil inside. Would you like for me to read the cards for you?"

I was speechless, shocked at what she said without me saying a word about the purpose for which I had come. My response was, "No, thank you. How much do I owe you? She replied, Nothing. Go fix up your marriage."

I did not realize at that time that God was answering my concern without me even knowing or paying attention to it. I left that office and immediately called my wife and told her I was not completely sure I wanted to move forward with the divorce. I told her I was confused and would not go to the appointment. My next call was to the other lady, to whom I said that what started as an adventure was getting too complex for me, and I was done. Instantly, she lost it and just went off on me. The devil showed his face through her. Little did I know that this would be only my first experience where God spoke to me loud and clear. Days later, I sat down with my wife to have a serious conversation about our lives and our relationship moving forward. She told me that she had been praying for me to reconsider and try to resolve our marriage. Well, it worked.

At that point, I had a job offer to move to South Florida for a business opportunity, and we both decided to move and get away from it all to rebuild our marriage and family. Little did I know the plans God had for us in the future.

We moved to Weston, Florida, in August 2014, and I started traveling for business. Even though I had been faithful to our marriage, I was still neglecting the family in the sense of not spending quality time with them and, instead, just concentrating on making money and taking care of business. I almost fell back into my old ways, but God is so good and faithful, and He was still reaching out for me to be able to fulfill my purpose in life.

> *If we say that we have no sin, we deceive ourselves, and the truth is not in us. If we confess our sins, He is faithful and just to forgive us our sins and to cleanse us from all unrighteousness. (1 John 1:8-9 NKJV)*

On April 13, 2015, I received a call from my boss at the time letting me know that they were restructuring and that I was out of a job. I will never forget that day. Usually, I could foresee this type of situation and always had a plan B up my sleeve to jump to the next project. This time I was caught unaware and felt completely lost. A deep depression overtook me, and all I did was get drunk, smoke, and hang out in the house pool all day for six months. As a result, I ended up losing everything. We sold our house in Puerto Rico in a short sale, moved from our rental property in Weston, and ended up living on borrowed money from family and friends. I started venturing into many different businesses and jobs as I told myself I would never work for corporate America again. After having lots of success, making lots of money, and being well-off, I started jumping from job to job, earning less than I did at my first job after college. I sold payroll services. Then I was a robotics operator. Sounds fancy, right? It was a disgusting job operating a camera that took pictures of sewers. I even delved into several network marketing businesses.

During my business ventures, my wife and I were invited to a comedy show. At the time, we were going crazy without purpose, not knowing what was next or what to do. So, we decided to go to see if at least we could laugh a little.

When we got to the location where the comedy show was, we realized it was a church. And it happened that the comedian was a pastor from Colombia. After his show, he gave his testimony, which included having a lot of success and traveling the world while neglecting his family. I completely related to his life and reflected on his testimony. After giving his testimony, he followed with a call to salvation. My hand and my wife's hand just raised by themselves as we gave our lives to Jesus for the first time ever. That is when I realized that God had been knocking on my door for the longest time, but I was not willing or wanting to listen. I understood then that God had been speaking to me ever since that weird visit to the fortune teller back in Puerto Rico and even on many occasions before that.

At that point, I decided I wanted to work for God. I wanted to give Him control of our lives and learn to walk with Jesus. The church where the comedy show was became our spiritual house. We have been going there ever since. We have gone through difficulties, but we have never let go of God, no matter what. We have learned and grown in our faith, and for the first time, we started to see opportunities and doors opening for us in a crazy way.

One of the opportunities that came from our relationships at the church was opening a security agency with several members of the congregation. This was an incredible opportunity for personal growth and to serve the security needs of churches. Then the pandemic hit, and the business closed. Everything stopped, but the bills kept coming. My wife and I had faith that God would provide, and we looked for ways to re-invent ourselves under our new circumstances. With God now in our hearts, we were not about to fall again, as we did before, so we started to look for things to do with our abilities.

Back in Puerto Rico, I participated in tactical shooting competitions and was a firearms hobbyist. So, with that background and all my security licenses and experience, we decided to open Right Way Firearms Academy. We concentrated on training families on safety and accident prevention. The business did very well and paid the bills for some time. However, other opportunities presented themselves, and we were always open to new things.

In a casual conversation, a good friend mentioned he had gone into handyman work and was having much success. I have always been very handy, to the point when I would visit friends and family, I would end up fixing something or installing something for them for beer and food. So, we looked into this business and decided to jump into the opportunity since everyone was locked up at home. We started doing many repairs, so we created Handyman PRO Solutions and got to work. My wife and I would go out every day to give service to many clients – we were The Dynamic Duo. And we had the best time of our lives despite it being hard and completely exhausting work.

God is good and faithful. He provided for us as we went into homes and worshipped as we worked, blessing our clients with high-quality work at a reasonable price. We always prayed to God to bring us help. If I had started this business when I was 25, it would have been amazing, but at my present age, not 25, it was getting overwhelming. I could only do what I could with my two hands and the knowledge God had given me. Clients often asked me to do bigger projects, but I could not get good people to help me. It was as if we had hit the ceiling and could not go beyond it.

There were times we bit off more than we could chew, and in those cases, my good friend and brother, Jose Ferrufino, would give us a hand. (Ferru, I love you!!) He would drive from Miami to Coral Springs (an hour and a half drive) after work at 6:00 pm to work with me until 11 or midnight, just to help me finish the work I did not have enough knowledge or experience to complete. He is a lifesaver. I told him that someday we would end up working together. Always trust and have faith in God.

> *Trust in the Lord with all your heart, and Lean not on your own understanding; In all your ways acknowledge Him, and He shall direct your paths. (Proverbs 3:5-6 NKJV)*

This has become my life verse. We knew God had something waiting for us, so we kept moving forward in faith. For many years I was invited to an event called Band of Brothers, but I always gave an excuse not to go. I was too ashamed to say it was because of financial issues. Well, guess what? I was invited again, and this time, I was ready. God's timing is perfect, so I went to the event, and it was amazing. I highly recommend it!

> But those who wait on the Lord Shall renew their strength; They shall mount up with wings like eagles, They shall run and not be weary, They shall walk and not faint. (Isaiah 40:31 NKJV)

Little did I know that my life would take a wild turn at this event. At Band of Brothers, I casually met Sean Loomis (Shout out to Seaney!!) at a dominos table, and I shared my testimony with him. As we continued speaking, he mentioned he had a friend who could benefit from our services, and we might be able to benefit from his business as well, so he would introduce us.

One week later, I received a call from Laurent Minguez (read his chapter in this book if you have not already) asking to meet and talk. The moment we met, it was as if I had known him for a long time. We shared so many things in common, especially our love for Christ and the willingness to give it all for Him and dedicate our lives to serving Him in every way we could. Laurent was my "brother from another mother." He was building a remodeling and construction company but was regularly getting scammed by contractors, so he was trying to grow a team from within. At that meeting on June 1, 2021, we agreed to take a month to put some teams together and then come back to the table to see what we could do.

That evening I received a call from Ferru telling me he had gotten fed up with his job and quit that day. He asked me what he should do. Talk about God's timing. I was so surprised I did not know what to say other than to tell him my wife and I were starting a three-day project the following day and that he should come work with us. I told him we would split the profits 50/50. So, we did. And to my surprise, we finished the entire project in one day. Talk about God speaking in mysterious ways. This was confirmation of what was about to happen. I picked up the phone and called Laurent. I told him that God did not want us to wait and that I already had a very productive team. That was the beginning of something wonderful and miraculous! We started working together and building what now is a conglomerate of businesses that point to the right owner of everything in this world - GOD.

> The earth is the Lord's, and all its fullness, The world and those who dwell therein. (Psalm 24:1 NKJV)

> "The Silver is Mine, and the gold is Mine," says the Lord. (Haggai 2:8 NKJV)

God has built a ministry in the marketplace that, at this point, is blessing over 60 families in several related industries. This story is being written even as we speak, so I will just have to save the rest of the story for another chapter.

Be Good
Be Safe
Be Blessed!!!

FAITH TO OVERCOME THE BLUES

Battling sadness, or having a case of the blues, is a problem many men face, and dealing with it can be scary. King David was troubled and battled deep despair, and Elijah was weary and afraid. Jonah was angry and wanted to run. Many strong men in the Bible show us that this struggle is real. After all, even Jesus wept in sadness. If you find yourself feeling down, take heart, there is hope. This verse reminds us that with God on our side, there is nothing to fear: *Fear not, for I am with you; Be not dismayed, for I am your God; I will strengthen you, Yes, I will help you, I will uphold you with My righteous right hand.* (Isaiah 41:10 NKJV)

> *Anxiety In the heart of man causes depression, but a good word makes it glad.* (Proverbs 12:25 NKJV)

We are emotional beings, and at times we all experience feelings of sadness and loss of interest. This affects how we feel, think, and behave and can lead to a variety of emotional and physical problems.

Something that can lead to a bout of blues may be a lack of hope. When we walk through life looking away from hope, our minds can become saturated with the weight of discouragement. Before we know it, we are drowning in the depths of sadness or grief. In His Word, God tells us that we can go to Him when we are weighed down.

> *"Come to me, all you who are weary and burdened, and I will give you rest. Take my yoke upon you, and learn from me, for I am gentle and humble in heart, and you will find rest for your souls. For my yoke is easy and my burden is light."* (Matthew 11:28-30 NIV)

When you are experiencing a depressed heart, look to the glory of Christ. God reminds us that He has shared the hope of glory, Jesus Christ, with us. (Colossians 1:27) The root of all joy is salvation! And we can all accept God's gift of salvation by asking forgiveness for our sins, believing Jesus died to pay the debt incurred by our sins, and confessing Jesus as Lord. Accepting salvation allows us to share in the eternal joy of living life with God forever.

If you are feeling down, identify the causes, and if that is difficult, ask God to reveal those causes to you. He will do this. It helps to know what you are fighting against, so you must take this to God in prayer. Then read the scriptures. Psalms is a beautiful place to go. All throughout the chapters, you will hear of ways to combat depressive thoughts. A great place to begin is Psalm 91. Let me encourage you to read the whole chapter.

God tells us in 1 Peter 5:7, *Cast all your anxiety on him because he cares for you.* (NIV)

Psalm 34:17-18 reminds us of God's heart and care for His children, no matter what they are going through. *The righteous cry out, and the Lord hears them; he delivers them from all their troubles. The Lord is close to the brokenhearted and saves the crushed in spirit.* (NIV)

Christians can take comfort in knowing that they do not suffer alone. There are men who will walk beside you and who are strong and faithful leaders of God. Find a band of brothers to walk through life with. Embrace men of honor who will point you to God. Surround yourself with leaders who are believers, and they will speak life into your life. There are groups that can encourage you, strengthen you, and empower you in our Lord. Do not isolate! When we attempt to walk alone, it is prime time for the enemy to attack. Please reach out to others when you feel yourself sinking into despair. Find yourself an accountability person who will read the scriptures with you, pray with you, and speak life into you in those moments when you feel sad or uninterested. You need a man of honor in these moments, one who is able and strong enough to help you. God has provided you, through this book, with many men who are willing warriors available to partner with you and gird you up with the armor it takes to fight through the struggle.

. . . .

MIGUEL LEWIS

Miguel Lewis, Psy.D, CGP, ABPP is a Clinical Psychologist at the West Palm Beach Veterans Hospital, where he provides individual, couples, and group therapy. He is a Certified Group Psychotherapist (CGP) and is Board Certified in Couples and Family Psychology (ABPP).

Miguel first heard of the Band of Brothers organization through one of his best friends, Kevin Hobbs. He has faithfully attended the Band of Brother's "Boot Camps," which ignited his passion for men's issues. Miguel is a proud member of the Band of Brother's Leadership Team, whose mission is to bring more men to the Lord.

Miguel is the husband of Blanca Lewis, his friendly and cheerful Latin wife of nearly 20 years. They are the parents of two lovely teenage daughters named Alyssa and Natalie. He is grateful for his brother and sister, Alex and Alessandra Lewis. Miguel credits his passion of tennis and learning to his father, and the importance of family, as well as his love of traveling, to his mother.

You can contact Miguel Lewis at Miguellew@gmail.com

FROM AN OPEN WOUND TO AN OPEN HEART

BY MIGUEL LEWIS

Fathers are important figures in the development of a boy. What can a son learn from his dad? In the words of John Eldridge, author of *Wild at Heart,* masculinity is bestowed. That is, "A boy learns how he is and what he's got from a man, or the company of men."[1] Yet, boys and men can be wounded by fathers who don't spend time with their sons, resulting in anger, inferiority, shame, unworthiness, and a host of other emotions. In this chapter, I will discuss how I was emotionally wounded by my father and how I overcame that adversity through faith in our Heavenly Father.

---

[1]   Eldridge, J. (2010) *Wild at Heart: Discovering The Secret of A Man's Soul.* HarperCollins Christian Publishing, Inc.

THE BEGINNING OF THE WOUND

About twelve years ago, I spoke about my father in my own group therapy. I opened up that I told my dad I didn't feel close to him, and he responded, "Let's go watch some tennis." I told the group I was upset with my dad for this suggestion as it was not what I wanted. Yet, a male in the group said something that made me think. "That was your father's way of getting close to you." Oops. Hearing that point made something shift in me at that moment. My father was attempting to get closer to me, yet I had been looking for a deeper connection.

Six years ago, the wound became clearer when I attended a four-day Band of Brothers yearly event entitled the "Boot Camp." This Christian men's event included a video by John Eldridge as he spoke about the wound. In addition, I heard other men speak about the wounds created by their fathers by not being there for them and not caring about their needs. During the quiet time in which we journaled, we were asked to answer questions about our own experiences, such as:

What did your father teach you as a boy?
What was your dad's message to you?
Do you know beyond a doubt he loved you?
Did he validate you in a hundred ways, saying, "You have what it takes?"

That was the first time I had thought about questions like those. I recently reviewed my written material from that Boot Camp and saw that, although I answered the first question, I responded to the second question with, "I don't know." And I answered the final two questions with a single word: "No." Then, at the end of the page, I wrote, "I am wounded by my father because he never said he loved me.

I have never felt close to him." There it was, the wound. Painful to write then and painful to read again.

As I was writing this chapter, I decided to review the texts between my father and me from the past few years. In January 2018, I attempted to connect with my father. Here is what I texted:

Me: *How are you? What about that meditation course I texted you? Yoga? Psychotherapy?*

I was worried about my father as he had seemed depressed. I didn't receive a response. So, I texted him the next day, and he responded by stating he was considering a therapist. So, then I texted him again.

Me: *Great news. I'm proud of you. I have been thinking of a father and son trip for a while now. I'll call you over the weekend so we can set up some dates. Sound okay?*

Dad: *No, not ready for that yet.*

Me: *Okay.*

That text was four years ago. I believe that's when the feelings of rejection started to grow. I wanted to connect with my father, and he "was not ready for that yet." It would even have been pleasing if he had stated, "Thank you," when I noted I was proud of him. That could have been an opportunity for us to connect. But he missed it.

Reviewing those texts, I found another occasion where I had reached out to my dad. I asked, in person, if he wanted to watch a live tennis tournament with me; he didn't respond. Instead, he froze. I inquired about his reaction in a text a day later, but he didn't respond. I then texted again and asked if he wanted to spend the night with mom at our house. He replied, "No thanks, but thanks for the invite." During this timeframe, I also asked him to attend our daughter's middle school graduation. No response. Attempt after attempt after attempt. I continually reached out to my father to have a relationship with him. And each time, I was rejected. The wound was gradually becoming worse.

On January 30th of this year, I sent my dad yet another text. It was then that the rejection started to become very painful. I could no longer blow it off or suppress it.

Me: *See the Raphael Nadal tennis match?*

Dad: *No. I just turned on the Tennis Channel and saw he won in five sets, his 21st Grand Slam.*

Me: *Yep. Watch it. Good stuff. My boy finally won another Australian.*

I had started off being friendly. When he responded, I went for it, making myself vulnerable. I was all in.

Me: *It's sad we don't see you and mom anymore. What's holding you back from moving closer to us?*

Dad: *Mom wants to move, but I'd rather not.*

At this point, my anger boiled as I was not getting what I wanted—a father who was involved with his grandchildren and me. It was as if a Sergeant in the Army, while in the middle of battle, was screaming, "Run, run! Sniper fire is coming in!" In the middle of that battle, with bullets flying, one hit me—right in the heart. After the smoke cleared, the Sergeant saw what occurred and yelled, "Man down!" And that man down was me. I was wounded...hurt... and alone.

Instead of responding to my father with tenderness, a place that is hard to react from as it is way too vulnerable, I did what many of us do. I got angry. I wanted to be real, so I texted:

Me: *You're not getting it or providing me an answer – all vague. Your son tells you to move closer and he has been trying to connect for years. Yet, you do same – remain distant. I don't get it. I would do anything for Alyssa and Natalie.*

Raw. Painful. I was pleading with my father. What I was really asking but not saying was, "Dad, do you love me? Will you fight for me? Am I important to you?"

Dad: *I hear you.*

Me: *Thanks.*

I was thinking to myself, *"I hear you?" That's it? I'm wounded, and that's the best he can come up with?* Feeling rejected and sensing I was not going to get what I wanted from him, I simply stated, "Thank you." I had to tend to my wounds all on my own.

One week later, on February 4th, I attempted one last time to connect with him. I texted him a video link of highlights from the recent Raphael Nadal tennis match. Tennis is our common ground, and we have always enjoyed talking about this sport.

Me: *Great highlights of Raphael Nadal. You can watch the whole Nadal vs. Medvedev match on YouTube.*

Dad: *I watch the summaries in the news.*

Me: *Okay.*

BOOM! Another shot to my heart. Man down, man down! The years of rejection had all boiled up in that moment. I was furious. There was heat in my body, my heart was beating wildly, and my mind was racing. I thought about texting him back and stating "ouch" or "rejected again." Yet, I couldn't risk being rejected any further. There was no more denying my pain or pushing it away. It was too much at that point, and I recalled being very angry and thinking, *You _ucking idiot. Don't you get it? Your son is trying to reach you. How about a thank you for sending me that text?* I was alone in my pain, all alone. I was hurt, felt rejected, angry, and helpless. I was lost—a terrible place for any man to be.

Yet, fortunately, in that moment, I realized I was not alone. God is always there right with us. And He got involved when I needed Him the most.

> *For where two or three gather in my name, there am I with them.* (Matthew 18:20 NIV)

I reached out by text to a group of ten guys from my Band of Brothers squad. This group meets every other Sunday online to have meetings where we share with one another. In that text, I stated I needed to have a Zoom call immediately, as I was hurting. It was 4:00 pm on a Friday, and many of the men were working, but fortunately, one man named Michael answered the text and was willing to have a Zoom call with me. He was patient, kind, and listened to me. I was no longer alone. Someone was there for me as I cried. I was so thankful that he, through God, helped soothe my anger. God guided me to be involved in this organization long ago as He knew I would need it at this moment. I had someone I could rely on, and it was all because of God.

> Get rid of all bitterness, rage and anger, brawling and slander, along with every form of malice. (Ephesians 4:31 NIV)

MY FATHER'S SLEEPING DISORDER

I think it is fair that if I talk about my wounds from my father, I should also explain what was occurring with him during the time frame of these texts. For the past five years, he had been affected by a sleeping disorder, which limits his sleep to only 3-4 hours a night. As a result, he slowly lost interest in many things he used to do. My father, who never had any longstanding feelings of depression and anxiety in his life, was now becoming totally different.

One day after the conversation with Michael, I decided to Google the effects of only receiving 3-4 hours of sleep daily. God was working on my heart and giving me wisdom. I learned that a lack of sleep causes depression. When I read that, it hit me like a ton of bricks. Depression. My father has depression. Now, I knew this already as my dad had changed over the years. He would no longer smile or laugh. He was no longer involved in the many activities he used to engage in, such as playing tennis, attending Rotary meetings, volunteering, playing poker, and reading. He even lost his sense of humor. Previously, he had been involved in life. Yet, all of that stopped when he started having sleep difficulties. Reading the word "depression" affected me profoundly. And at the same time, I thought, *Here I am, wanting more from my father.* In that moment, God helped me understand my father. The Lord told me I was asking for something that was not possible at that time. My dad had enough occurring just getting through the day. Every day was a struggle for him. I then had a newfound sense of compassion for my father.

> *Be kind and compassionate to one another, forgiving each other, just as in Christ God forgave you.* (Ephesians 4:32 NIV)

THE AFTERMATH

A few months later, in another squad meeting, an additional big shift occurred. As I spoke about my concern over my father's lack of sleep, Michael expressed, "Hey, you are no longer angry at your father." I was surprised by this observation, but he was correct. I was lighter and didn't have all that bitterness in my heart. I had forgiven my father without even realizing it.

> *Bear with each other and forgive one another if any of you has a grievance against someone. Forgive as the Lord forgave you.* (Colossians 3:13 NIV)

God was working on me. He had turned my bitterness into compassion, allowing me to let go of my pain and release it to God. Finally, I was free—and that felt good.

Shortly after my newfound realization that I had compassion in my heart and had forgiven my father, I stayed the night with my parents. Now, being a husband and a father of two, I usually visit my parents with my family in tow. But this time I went alone. As I spent time with just my parents, I felt like I did when I was younger. It was special with just the three of us.

That evening, my father and I watched *Jeopardy* and a documentary about Hemingway. I learned my father enjoyed Hemingway's writing. My father told me that he thought Hemingway's life, filled with travel, was interesting. In those moments, I was learning what my father's interests were. And I also realized I was bonding with my father and obtaining what I was looking for long ago—time with him.

REMEMBERING MY FATHER'S CARE

Something changed in my life when I forgave my father and released my wound to God. I became free and cared more deeply for my father. Then, I was able to recall three important moments in my life when my father had been there for me when I needed him.

In my 20s, I was let go from my first job after only nine months. That was a painful period for me as I, at times, felt sadness and shame for being unemployed. Without work, I had lost my identity. Seeing that I lacked direction, my father suggested that I learn Spanish and offered to pay for a trip to Latin America. I took him up on that offer, leaning into my new purpose as I studied Spanish in Antigua, Guatemala. I am thankful for my father as I not only learned Spanish, but I met wonderful people and lived with a Guatemalan family. And when I returned? I found work in a great organization called Big Brother and Big Sisters – a perfect fit for me at that time. My father was there for me.

In my later 20s, I applied to graduate schools in Clinical Psychology, and I was disappointed I did not get into my top choice—Rutgers University. Yet, my father told me that learning does not stop in graduate school. Rather, one can continue to learn no matter what graduate school one attends. I embraced this as I became trained in group therapy as well as Acceptance and Commitment Therapy and obtained board certification in couple and family psychology. All after graduate school. My father was there for me.

And a few years ago, my father was very patient with me as I was going through tough times at work. It was a stressful period for me as I feared I could lose my job. Every day was a struggle. And when I spoke to my father about it, I didn't need a lecture or criticism. And he didn't provide either. Rather, he was simply supportive and listened. My father was there for me.

WHAT I LEARNED FROM MY FATHER

My forgiveness and compassion for my father also helped me recognize and celebrate what I learned from him over the years.

My father introduced me to many things, shaping who I became. He introduced me to Boy Scouts, where I later became an Eagle Scout, the highest rank in Boy Scouts. He played tennis with me, which is a sport I play to this day. My father also showed me what is important in life. He didn't drive a fancy car, didn't wear brand-named clothing, and we didn't have a fancy house. Instead, he and my mother spent money on vacations. And I am proud to say, as a father, this is a tradition in my family as well. I learned from my father the importance of going to a small university as opposed to a big one. As a result, I went to Rollins College, where I played tennis, was involved in a jazz band, and joined a fraternity, all while reaping the benefits of a school with only 1800 students. Lastly, my father showed me the importance of valuing different cultures as he not only married my mother, who is from Puerto Rico, but he and my mother adopted two children from Brazil. I learned from my father.

This reflection helped me realize I am very much like my father. I drive an old car just like he did because a newer one is just not important to me. I went to a small university like him, and now I am encouraging my daughter to consider a small university as well. I am also well-rounded like he was. He played tennis, was involved in Rotary, played guitar, volunteered, and enjoyed other cultures. I play tennis, am involved in a community organization, play the saxophone, and enjoy other cultures. And I married a Latin woman. I learned from my father.

God healed me from my bitterness, and I now have compassion and love for my father. Today I can say I am grateful for my father because I am the man I am today because of him. I have gone from bitterness to gratitude, from anger to compassion, and from feeling distant to feeling closer. And it was all because God led me to become involved in the Band of Brothers organization, which helped me through those specific moments when I was hurting. God has always been there for me.

HEALED IN LOVE

On July 10th of this year, I asked my squad this question, "How do I write a chapter about my wounds from my father without wounding my father in the process?" I was nervous and worried about the impact on him. One group member told me that although his own father wounded him, he did not address it before his father passed away. His point was that although it may be painful for my father to read this chapter, he needs to hear how he wounded me so healing can occur. I proudly stated to him that I was already healed. I had forgiven my dad. Another squad member then brought to my attention that my chapter would change men's lives. This provided me with peace in the midst of all my worries. These powerful words of support from other men filled my soul and felt good. Then, with tears in my eyes and a lump in my throat, I stated to the group, "I love my father."

From bitterness to gratitude, from anger to compassion, and from distance to feeling closer. And finally, from an open wound to an open heart filled with love. God showed up that evening in the squad, just as He always does—just as He has through all my moments of pain. And through Him, I overcame my adversity through faith.

FAITH TO OVERCOME ANXIETY

Anxiety is triggered by so many things and becomes a crisis when it interferes with our faith. Anxiety's presence in our life shows that a person has not been able to put their full trust in God. God tells us in His Word that we are not to be fearful, especially when we see things are not going our way—many things are beyond our control anyway. When anxiety develops, we should immediately relinquish it by taking it to God in prayer, thanksgiving, and worship. When we trust Him, He takes over, because in obedience we brought the situation before Him and surrendered it to Him in prayer.

> Do not be anxious about anything but in every situation, by prayer and petition, with thanksgiving, present your requests to God. (Philippians 4:6 NIV)

The devil uses our flaws to break us down, and he doesn't want us reliant on God. The more we are filled with anxiety, the less we are filled with God's Word and His Spirit. Our Father knows our needs and takes care of them. Putting God first is a cure for anxiety.

Anxiety can often result from sin in our life, so it is important to make sure we deal with sin. When sin is confessed to God, we are forgiven, and the heavy weight of guilt is taken away.

Blessed is the one whose transgressions are forgiven,
whose sins are covered.
Blessed is the one whose sin the Lord does not count
against them and in whose spirit is no deceit.
When I kept silent, my bones wasted away through
my groaning all day long.
For day and night your hand was heavy on me;
my strength was sapped as in the heat of summer.
Then I acknowledged my sin to you and did not cover
up my iniquity.
I said, "I will confess my transgressions to the Lord."
And you forgave the guilt of my sin.
(Psalm 32:1-5 NIV)

Turn the situation that caused your anxiety over to God. He is in control of it all. So often, our anxiety rises because we want perfection and fall short of that perfect "mind picture"—how we expect things to look, who we think we should be, or even what we want or feel entitled to have. Are there overwhelming circumstances of imperfection plaguing you right now, causing anxiety in your life? Have faith in God. As long as we are with Jesus, we have nothing to fear. Jesus is perfect, and we can count on Him to provide for our needs, protect us from evil, and keep our souls secure for eternity.

None of our imperfections matter to God. Being a child of God is what matters! With practice, prayer, and help from God, the battle can be won, or at the very least, the anxiety can be made manageable. Look to God alone for validation and forgiveness, strength and reliance.

We can see the example God gave us in Matthew 8:23-27, where we read about Jesus' disciples as they became distressed in a heavy storm. Jesus rebuked their lack of faith. Then He rebuked the wind and the waves.

When your storm rises up, skip the part where you become stressed or anxious and, instead, go right to God for His help. Rebuke the wind and waves that come against you just as Jesus did. You have that power and authority as a Man of God. You may not be able to control the anxious thoughts from entering your mind, but you can practice the right response. The more we become aware of His presence and trust His Holy Spirit to carry us through challenging encounters, the less we become victimized by anxiety. Allow God to bring healing to your trauma and truth to any falsehoods you may have.

> Do not be anxious about anything, but in every situation, by prayer and petition, with thanksgiving, present your request to God. And the peace of God which transcends all understanding, will guard your hearts and your minds in Christ Jesus. (Philippians 4:6-7 NIV)

The scripture that follows your act of obedience when the anxiety hits is Philippians 4:7. God's Word tells us that peace floods in after you pray with thanksgiving. You are loved, you are accepted, and you are not created to be full of fear. God's Word tells us to be strong in the Lord and in the strength of His might and put on the whole armor of God so you can stand against the schemes of the devil. The battle rages with anxiety, but you have a means to an end!

For we do not wrestle against flesh and blood, but against the rulers, against the authorities, against the cosmic powers over this present darkness, against the spiritual forces of evil in the heavenly places. Therefore take up the whole armor of God, that you may be able to withstand in the evil day, and having done all, to stand firm. Stand therefore, having fastened on the belt of truth, and having put on the breastplate of righteousness, and, as shoes for your feet, having put on the readiness given by the gospel of peace. In all circumstances take up the shield of faith, with which you can extinguish all the flaming darts of the evil one; and take the helmet of salvation, and the sword of the Spirit, which is the word of God, praying at all times in the Spirit, with all prayer and supplication. (Ephesians 6:12-18 ESV)

. . . .

JACK SAPOLSKY

Jack Sapolsky was born 05 May 1955; his mother knew he wasn't going to be very sharp, so she gave him an easy one. Raised in The Bronx, N.Y., in a broken home (which at that time and era wasn't too popular), Jack decided to leave the formal education system for that of experience. His occupational travels went from grocery store delivery boy to construction work, auto mechanic, butcher, and, believe it or not, to being a well-respected Financial Coach for the last 38+ years with the largest financial services company in North America. Jack has helped thousands of families become debt free, properly protected, and financially independent. As of May 2022, Jack has $668,512,186 of Individual Term Life Insurance issued, paid $19,028,219 in Death Claims to beneficiaries, and his clients have more than $158,157,243 in mostly Retirement Assets Under Management. (Only by the grace of GOD, Jack finally passed his Securities exam only after 6 attempts!) Jack gives ALL Glory to GOD. (Zechariah 4:6: *Not by might nor by power, but by My spirit.* NKJV) Additionally, Jack successfully coaches others to coach others from coast to coast.

IN SEARCH OF ANSWERS

BY JACK SAPOLSKY

So, here I am, sitting at my desk at home with my hands in my face trying to figure out how I'm going to put into words what my great friend Ken Hobbs II asked me to do – to tell you my story and what I've learned along the way.

I have no idea where to begin other than the beginning. At this point in my life, I was NOT a Man of Honor, not even close. My goal and prayer is to give hope and inspiration to all who read this. My message is to never give up hope and always be curious and ask questions. The answers will show you the way. No matter how much trouble you get in.

With that said, here we go...

I was born and raised in the South Bronx in the mid-fifties, my mom and dad got divorced when I was four years old, and my baby brother was four months old. That meant my mom had to go to work every day, traveling by subway from the Bronx to Manhattan and leaving me to be raised by the superintendent of the building. José and his wife spoke no English, but we did the best we could to communicate.

That lack of supervision and direction left me to be influenced and essentially raised by the "streets." To borrow a title from a book, "Down these Mean Streets" is an appropriate description of my life growing up - hanging out with the "wrong" crowd and always getting in trouble. The only direction was the wrong direction, as I looked to the wrong people for leadership.

I was brought up with my mom and grandmother, both of the Jewish faith. My grandmother was very traditional, very old-school, and wanted me to carry on those traditions, so I was forced to attend Hebrew school. To say I rebelled is an understatement, but to make grandma happy, I went. While there, however, I questioned the Rabbi about some Jewish religious traditions, which caused me to wonder if there was more to the story. More on that later.

Like all my educational experiences, I hated Hebrew school and cut as often as possible. Then, I would break into the mailbox to get the notices sent home about my absences before my mom could read them. I did this so often that I was held back in 10th grade three times. I think my yearbook should have read "What Jack will be when he graduates is old." So I quit school altogether.

Again, this resulted in my hanging out in the streets and getting in trouble - more trouble than I'm willing to talk about here.

I ran away from home at the age of 14. I went to a friend's house who lived on Long Island and started to learn to be an auto mechanic, which would become my first trade.

Once again, the only leadership I had to follow was bad leadership. So much so that my mom signed me up for a 4-year hitch in the United States Marine Corps at 16 years old during Vietnam time. How desperate was she to help me find my way?

Think about it. I went from being a bad kid, with no leadership or discipline, to being a young man with a rifle in his hands, being taught how to kill. It was quite the irony. But there was much I learned in the Marines that would be instrumental in my life. I learned to respect others and how to be a man and a leader. I also learned how to take orders and do what I was told when I was told to do it. I learned my actions had consequences; I learned about honor and loyalty. And I learned how to pray. All of those things taught me how to overcome adversity through faith.

I discovered I like to learn - and there was so much to learn.

I remember going to my family's house in Brooklyn for the Jewish holidays, such as Passover. We would go through the religious rituals, like hiding the matzoh and leaving the front door open, waiting for or inviting the Messiah to come. I always wanted to know more. I discovered that the "Matzoh" was called "Afikomen" (the Greek meaning for "I have come"). Still, I had more questions, and I wanted to know the answers. There had to be more answers.

In 1976 I got married at the ripe old age of 21. My new wife and I packed up all our things, loaded them in a U-Haul, and headed from Long Island, New York, to South Florida. We got off the highway on Commercial Boulevard in Fort Lauderdale because it sounded good. We had no place to live, no job, and no direction. All we had were our hopes and dreams.

We had a daughter in 1981, and then we had another daughter who passed away a few years later.

Sometimes, things don't work out the way you plan. When that happens, you can choose how to respond. You can get bitter and complain, play the blame game, or go on.

In 1978, some good friends of mine, Sal and Theresa, were visiting. He asked me a provocative question, "Jack, if you died tonight, are you going to heaven?"

I answered, "I hope so."

And then he asked me, "Would you like to know for sure?"

Using a New American Standard Bible, Sal led me down "Romans Road."

- Romans 3:23 - *For all have sinned and fall short of the glory of God.*

- Romans 6:23 - *For the wages of sin is death, but the gracious gift of God is eternal life in Christ Jesus our Lord.*

- Romans 5:8 - *But God demonstrates His own love towards us, in that while we were yet sinners, Christ died for us.*

- Romans 10:9 - *That if you confess with your mouth Jesus as Lord, and believe in your heart that God raised Him from the dead, you will be saved.*

The questions I had all along were being answered. There was more to the story! I always knew in my heart there was an instruction book for the way we were to live our lives. There it all was - in the Bible.

One of the things I learned I found in the book of Ephesians (6:10-20). These verses made it clear to me that the devil is coming! I discovered that although those who have given their lives to Christ are firmly in the Lord's grips, the devil still tries to come after them. And he really goes after those who have not yet given their lives to Christ. The WAR is ON! Being a Marine, I was ready. Bring it.

Once a Marine, always a Marine. Once saved, always saved! (Romans 8:35-39)

Decades have gone by since Sal first walked me toward Christ, and thank you, Lord, I am a much better man than I could have been without you. You have given me strength beyond my wildest imagination. Those who hope in the Lord will renew their strength. *They will soar on wings like eagles; they will run and not grow weary, they will walk and not be faint.* (Isaiah 40:31 NIV)

For years, I've surrounded myself with people I want to be more like. And I've spent time reading and learning. At one point, I concluded that there are instruction books for almost everything in life except for how to live life. But I was wrong.

The instruction book on how to live life was, is, and always will be the Bible.

THE BIBLE'S INSTRUCTIONS ON LEADING

One of my goals was always to become a good leader. I believe becoming a good leader requires first becoming a good follower. That is a great place to start, but I wanted to go deeper. Looking for a plan to follow to become the leader I wanted to be brought me to Numbers 2:1-34.

Moses was a good planner and organizer (despite taking 40 years to take a 4-day trip).

Here are 12 points I took away from Numbers that have become essential in my walk with the Lord, my personal life, and my business life.

1. Planning is paramount.

2. As you plan, set the intended goal and focus on it.

3. As any good Marine will tell you, thoroughly evaluate the circumstance.

4. Decide on what is necessary to enact the plan.

5. Consider questions, and don't be afraid to ask them.

6. Be clear. Communicate, communicate, communicate.

7. Identify obstacles that may come against you. Beware, the devil is coming.

8. Be flexible and open to God's leading. Goals in stone, plans in sand.

9. Utilize schedules. Overbooking can be more effective than underbooking.

10. Budget realistically.

11. As you go, monitor your progress and allow God to guide your steps.

12. Evaluate the results.

THE BIBLE'S INSTRUCTIONS ON SOWING SEEDS

Applying the 12 points above each time you plant seeds of salvation, grow relationships, or nurture the expansion of business can help you become a leader and achieve purposeful progress.

Speaking of seeds, I am an avid believer in the "Law of the Seed," which says, *Sow, then reap. You cannot reap what you do not sow.* In other words, what you grow depends on what you plant.

Tommy Newberry writes in his book *Success is not an Accident:*

"Success is a planned outcome, not an accident. Success and failure are both predictable because they follow the natural and indisputable Law of Sowing and Reaping. Success is not based on need it is based on seed."[1]

Not only must we sow the correct type of seed, however, but for it to thrive, we must plant seeds in optimal conditions. Jesus teaches us this lesson in The Parable of the Sower.

---

[1]   Newberry, *Tommy. Success is Not an Accident.* Tyndale House Publishers 1999.

> "Listen! Behold, a sower went out to sow. And it happened, as he sowed, that some seed fell by the wayside; and the birds of the air came and devoured it. Some fell on stony ground, where it did not have much earth; and immediately sprang up because it had no depth of earth. But when the sun was up it was scorched, and because it had no root it withered away. And some seed fell among thorns; and the thorns grew up and chocked it, and it yielded no crop. But other seed fell on good ground and yielded a crop that sprung up, the crop increased and produced: some thirty-fold, some sixty, and some a hundred." (Mark 4:3-8 NKJV)

Here are eight things I learned while studying the Lord's instructions for seed-planting:

1. A lot of seeds must be scattered to produce a crop.

2. Not all soils produce, but we cannot reap if we do not sow.

3. We must continue sowing, trusting that one day we will reap a harvest.

4. Healthy soil that produces will multiply, and we will reap more than we sow.

5. We will reap in proportion to what we have sown.

6. We can't do anything about last week's harvest, but we can always sow more seeds this week.

7. We must believe in the seed we sow, trusting that some will produce fruit.

8. Once we see fruit, all our efforts seem worthwhile.

THE BIBLE'S INSTRUCTIONS ON DECISIONS AND CONSEQUENCES

Leviticus 26:3-39 teaches us about decisions and consequences. Leadership, like life, is the sum of the decisions we make. Every decision has consequences; how we respond to people matters. We decide what values are worth going to the mat for.

In this scripture, God lists the blessings He offers those who obey Him and the punishment we will receive for disobedience. God, the ultimate Leader, clearly outlines the consequences of His people's choices.

Studying this part of God's instruction book opened my eyes to some of my past failures.

1. I lacked commitment.

2. I suffered from a scattered focus.

3. I looked for excuses.

4. I forget the big picture.

5. I'd go public with private thoughts.

6. I adapted the motto, "That's good enough."

7. I didn't take God's direction seriously.

8. I behaved inconsistently.

9. I created poor relationships.

10. I avoided change.

My prayer, as I list some of my own shortcomings with transparency, is that you will look at your own life, leadership, and decisions and ask God what He wants you to repent from and do differently going forward.

Today, I truly regret some of the things I have done, but I am forgiven, and I have forgiven myself. And I am much more aware of the choices and decisions I make.

LEADING INCLUDES LEANING – ON GOD, HIS PEOPLE, AND HIS WORD

I have been blessed with great friends and mentors, a great business, and a great relationship with my Father in heaven (and I don't mean my biological father.) I don't take any of that for granted, and I never stop striving to learn to lead well – recognizing that God teaches us in so many ways. I'd like to close with some thoughts I keep close as I journey through life.

- We are who we hang out with. So be intentional about the people you are around and be aware of how you are changing them or they are changing you.

- As John Maxwell has taught me, anyone can steer the ship, but it takes a leader to chart the course.[2] People won't do

---

2 Maxwell, John. *21 Indisputable Laws of Leadership*. Harper Collins, 1998.

what they hear, they will do what they see. Put another way by the founder of my company: leadership is everything.

- People don't plan to fail; they fail to plan. So, plan your work and work your plan. Day by day, one day at a time, get better and be better.

- Faith usually makes sense in reverse. Looking back and analyzing what I've gone through has enabled me to say, "That makes sense." Evaluating and remembering God's provision as I go through life always increases my faith.

- God wants us to come to Him prayerfully as we lead. I often pray 1 Chronicles 4:10 – widely known as The Prayer of Jabez: *And Jabez called on the God of Israel saying, "Oh, that you would bless me indeed, and enlarge my territory, that Your hand would be with me, and that You keep me from evil, that I may not cause pain!"* (NKJV)

A note on that last point: God granted Jabez what he requested. So PLEASE be careful what you ask for!

Thank you, Lord! I am so truly grateful as, at last, I am on the road to proudly becoming a United Man of Honor! If you or someone you know has lost their way or just hasn't found it yet, don't give up. Be curious, ask questions, and seek answers. Remember, Jesus is ALWAYS the answer. May GOD bless.

FAITH TO OVERCOME TEMPTATION

Temptation is something we all face, whether it comes at us from the world, the flesh, or directly from the enemy. One of the greatest temptations we face is thinking we can manage anything in this life on our own. We can all investigate our past to find something we wish we could change—perhaps something we fell into because we relied on our own strength and tried to navigate life without God's help. No matter how long we have been a believer, we are faced with temptations. And when we try to stand against those temptations alone, we usually mess up. But, the Bible gives us hope. Instead of choosing to sin (and temptation is NOT a sin), God always provides an escape from temptation. It is up to us whether or not we choose to overcome it.

There are strategies that you can use in your faith to help you combat tempting situations. First, it is crucial to understand, as Paul tells us in 1 Corinthians 10:13 (NLT), *the temptations in your life are no different from what others experience. And God is faithful. He will not allow the temptation to be more than you can stand. When you are tempted, he will show you a way out so that you can endure.* God will always give you a way to manage when situations arise and you are weak.

A great way to battle temptation is using your sword, the Word of God! It is what Jesus used to silence the enemy. Satan tempted Jesus in the wilderness with his appetite and emotions as he saw where circumstances had, perhaps, made Jesus weak. But Jesus used a repellent against the lies that the enemy was bombarding Him with—the Word of God. By using this sword that we all possess, Jesus overcame the tempter and shut down the devil.

Temptations can be intense, but that does not mean they have to overtake you. If someone tells you to drink poison, and you, being thirsty, take a sip believing the lie that the poison will actually make you feel good, make no mistake, your struggles will begin. You will begin to wrestle and wonder if, this time, the poison will kill you. The battle is real when you play with temptations. When you find yourself tempted, be honest before God. See the poison for what it is—deadly! Tell God you need Him. Tell Him you are having a tough time overcoming your temptation. Cry out to God, pray, and let Him rescue you. Then, find an accountability partner who knows what you struggle with. Confide in them and ask them to be there for you when temptations arise.

Please understand the most important thing for you to know is that God will never tempt you to do anything wrong. The devil and our flesh, which is sinful, tempt us to do wrong; but God never will. Sometimes God allows us to get into situations where we must make a choice between right and wrong, but just as Jesus passed the test by confronting the devil's lies with the truth of God's Word, we must do the same.

> *And remember, when you are being tempted, do not say, "God is tempting me." God is never tempted to do wrong, and he never tempts anyone else. (James 1:13 NLT)*

Pray that pride will not hold you back from looking to God for His help. As we look to God's Word to give us the truth, we need to fight the temptations we battle daily, and one of the greatest truths is that God will forgive any of us who have fallen if we trust Christ for forgiveness. It may take digging back to incidents you fell prey to in order to see where extreme guilt took hold. You may still hold on to guilt, shame, or pride because you knew you messed up in your life, making it easier to be tempted and fall again if it is not dealt with. Trust Christ alone for your salvation. When you confess your sin outright before Him, He forgives every fall into temptation.

God wants us to give our battles to Him daily. He does not want us to be alienated from Him. Walking with God every day helps us to find the strength to meet life's challenges, overcome adversity, and claim victory over temptation. You win the war against temptation by giving it to God and not fighting alone—remember, you have a band of brothers to help hold you up.

· ·

JULIO ANTA

Julio Anta is the head of the Safety (Security) Team Ministry at his church, Casa De Alabanza, Miami. He also leads a Band of Brothers Squad Men's Ministry for CDA Miami.

Anta is a retired corrections officer and Florida Department of Law Enforcement instructor. He was honorably discharged from the United States Marine Corps Reserves.

Julio has been teaching martial arts at Anta's Fitness and Self Defense since 1998. He holds multiple black belts. Anta is a former bodybuilding champion. You can see his training videos on www.youtube.com/antafit

An NRA gun and rifle instructor and Israeli tactical gun and rifle shooting instructor, Julio is also certified for and has done numerous self-defense, police defensive tactics, active shooter response, church safety team training, child safety, and anti-bullying workshops for numerous corporations, schools, and clubs.

Julio is the author of *Anta's Ageless Warrior Fitness* and designs and owns *Iron Patriot By Anta*, a Christian, patriotic apparel company, which can be accessed at www.ironpatriotbyanta.com.

Learn more about Julio on his websites: www.antamartialarts.com and www.doralkravmga.com.

FROM CHARLIE BROWN TO SUPERMAN

BY JULIO ANTA

Most of my success has come after I became born again. Satan had taken everything I valued from me, and I was in the biggest hole in my life. That was when I truly came to Christ in my heart. It was 1986. My story, my journey to Christianity, started in 1980. I went from being agnostic to believing in Jesus Christ ironically in what is coined "The Land That God Forgot."

I heard Pastor Bobby Cruz preach that when you give everything to God, He will give you back more than you had before. Deuteronomy 30:3 says, *Then the Lord your God will restore your fortunes and have compassion on you and gather you again from all the nations where he scattered you.* (NIV) Pastor Bobby was on top of his world, known as the King of Salsa. When he was born again, he stopped singing for the world, gave all his money to the church, and gave himself 100%

to Christ. He went from riches and fame to rags. Later God gave him back everything he had lost plus much more. My story is similar. What Satan took from me, God restored. And He gave me back so much more. I overcame adversity through faith.

I came to America three weeks before my 5th birthday, 1962, from the oppressed communist country of Cuba. At first, we lived in Miami Beach. Then we moved to Yonkers, New York, as there weren't many job opportunities in South Florida for my father.

At a very young age, I told my dad I wanted to look like the actor Steve Reeves who played Hercules, and I wanted to be a black belt. I was a small, sick kid who got bad grades. I was the last one picked in sports, and my self-esteem was very low. I commiserated and identified with Charlie Brown.

When I was around five years old, I took a vaccine and went into anaphylaxis shock. Then, because I started suffering from allergies, my allergist suggested we move back to Florida. Living in Miami Springs from junior high through high school and college, I followed the ways of the world and became super liberal and agnostic. Imagine how my parents felt, who had left communism, at my turn toward society.

In the winter of 1980, I enlisted in the Marine Corps Reserves. Before I went to boot camp, I met a guy who had been in the United States Marine Corps (USMC); he had enlisted to avoid prison. He told me how hard it was to survive USMC boot camp and that when I got there, I would read the Bible. This guy was not even a Christian or living a godly life when he told me this. I laughed, thinking it was a joke. Then, on December 2, 1980, I arrived at boot camp, and it was hell. They call the Marine Corps boot camp in Parris Island, South

Carolina, "the land that God forgot." Yet, that is where I started believing in God again. I got my Bible and read it every day. I did not miss a Sunday of church. I promised God that if I made it through boot camp, I would never miss a Sunday in church. When I graduated, however, I did not return to church. But at least I had my faith back.

In 1982, I had a medical issue that scared me. I went to the bathroom to do number two, and blood came out. Even though this had happened once before, I panicked, thinking something was terribly wrong. The incident drove me to turn the television to the Christian station, and I accepted the Lord Jesus Christ. I had been bodybuilding since 1976, and some of my bodybuilding friends had recently accepted the Lord and begun attending church. So, the next day I called my friend Ricardo Velez and told him what had happened, and he invited me to church. My parents were not happy with my decision to go. My mom was a devoted Catholic who planned to be a nun until my dad got in the way, and my father was more into idol worshiping. My mom called one of my Marine Corps friends to talk to me. He told me how concerned my parents were and that he knew I was not happy. I then spent the next three months going to church, but I backslid. I knew I needed a relationship with Jesus Christ, yet I did not want to give up my life of iniquity. My world was partying, womanizing, bodybuilding, and going to the beach.

I was a very shy guy and a slow muscle gainer. Yet, I was getting bigger by now, and my body had become my facade. Girls would come to me and start conversations. My life consisted of going to the disco club on Wednesday, Friday, Saturday, and Sunday; to the beach on Saturday and Sunday; and to the gym Monday through Friday. I couldn't hold a good, steady job because of my lifestyle. I began competing in bodybuilding in 1983 and placed 3rd in both Miami and Jr Florida Bodybuilding Championships. In 1985, I placed 4th in the Orange Classic.

I put together a bodybuilding show, and we would perform in disco clubs, at parties and events, and in the Collegian Bodybuilding Nationals. Life was what I dreamed of since I was a small child: girls, muscles, and fame. In those three years, however, my faith continued to backslide, and I was sinning more than ever. The Bible says in Mathew 12:43-45, *When an impure spirit comes out of a person, it goes...and takes with it seven other spirits more wicked than itself, and they go in and live there. And the final condition of that person is worse than the first.* (NIV)

I started doing martial arts again while I continued bodybuilding. I had done martial arts on and off, yet bodybuilding was my love and priority. I entered a tournament in 1986, and while sparring, I partially dislocated my shoulder. I continued to fight and then partially dislocated my other shoulder. I still continued to fight. When your adrenaline is going, you don't feel the pain. When the match was over, I was in so much pain that I couldn't take my uniform top off to change.

This started a series of trials in my life. First, I was told I should never lift weights or do martial arts again because my shoulders would get worse. A few weeks later, I went to the gym and discovered there were a lot of exercises I couldn't do. My facade, my body was now shrinking. Next, my girlfriend, who said she was a white witch (imagine that—a guy who had accepted the Lord ended up with a witch), came into the liquor store where I worked and started arguing with me, causing me to lose my job. Then, behind my back, she started seeing one of my bodybuilding friends who was also in my bodybuilding show, and she broke up with me. Then, to top it off, my car blew its engine. I thought that I was living a great life before this happened. Yet, I was a complete failure living in iniquity and sin. I was feeling depressed looking at my life—no car, no job, no girlfriend, losing my body, and living with my parents at 29 years old.

By now, my mom and dad were going to a Christian church. Even though I had backslid, I had planted the seed in my family. My mom told me about this cute "Chinese-looking" girl in church—Cubans call all Asians "Chinese." I dismissed this because I had never dated anyone my mom suggested.

The Monday after the 4th of July, 1986, I told my mom I wanted to go to church with her. From there, there was no turning back. I feared going back into the world and my old lifestyle and decided instead of the world, I would count on God. When calculating how long I've been a Christian, I don't count my encounters before this time because I was not born again; yet, I know God had His hand on me. My true walk with Christ began in 1986.

When you give your life to God, He will return to you way better things than you could imagine. I prayed that the next woman who came into my life would be my wife forever. I also always dreamed of marrying a virgin. Then, I met my wife Elena in church in 1986. She was that "Chinese-looking" girl, even though she wasn't Chinese but Hispanic. That was the first time I dated someone my mom suggested—I guess mother knows best.

My wife was the first and only person I dated since I truly gave my heart to Christ. My pastor, Bobby Cruz, preached about the importance of not having sex while dating. He told us how much more we would trust each other if we restrained. Elena and I dated for almost three years, and we did what the Bible says and did not have a sexual relationship until we got married in 1989. The Lord answered my prayer; I married a virgin wife. 1 Corinthians 7:28 NIV says, *But if you do marry, you have not sinned; and if a virgin marries, she has not sinned. But those who marry will face many troubles in this life, and I want to spare you this.* That decision is what helped me become a Man of Honor. Our dating life revolved around church ministries. We have been married for 33 years, together for 36 years since we started dating. God has blessed us with two sons, both married and successful, and one grandson.

After becoming a Christian, my life changed. All I wanted was to learn more about God. I still don't understand in a carnal sense why my wife started dating me or what she saw in me. I was broke, devastated, and depressed from everything that had happened to me. I recently asked her what she saw in me. She answered, "You had a nice face, didn't drink, had parents who were married, and you were a Christian." We know it was God's perfect plan.

Early in our relationship, I worked as a security guard in a mall, then at Radio Shack, although I was not a good salesman. As a result, we were broke in our first year of marriage. Our power was even shut off at times because we couldn't pay the bill on time. In 1989 while still working in Radio Shack, I reenlisted in the USMC Reserves with the rank I had left with—Sergeant. As a Christian, I was no longer doing the crazy and rowdy things I had earlier as a Marine. Instead, I ministered to many Marines, going from being a squad leader to platoon leader—a platoon is made up of three squads. I was also awarded the Naval

Achievement Medal for my leadership skills. I felt God was honoring me with success.

In September 1990, I was hired as a corrections officer at South Florida Corrections Center. Having an open contract in the Marine Corps, I left to focus on my studies in the academy, training for my new career. Since I have a bad memory and attention deficit disorder, I feared failing and being forced to return to Radio Shack, so I often stayed after class to study with a classmate. Because of my dedication and Marine Corps background, they saw leadership qualities in me and appointed me as a section leader. I was put in charge of half of my academy class, and for the first time in my life, I got the highest grade in a subject. I also tied for the highest grade in my first responder course.

Within a year and a half of working at the prison, I earned an administration job, which included having weekends and holidays off. I worked there for ten years, from 1990 to 2000. I was finally succeeding and overcoming adversity through my faith.

In 1990, before I started in the academy, I had begun taking martial arts more seriously. In 1992, I started training in Hung Gar Kung Fu. Then, in 1997 a Christian friend working at the prison taught me something that transformed my life. Habakkuk 2:2-3 says, *And the Lord answered me and said, Write the vision, and make it plain upon tables, that he may run and readeth it. For the vision is yet for an appointed time, but at the end it shall speak, and not lie: though it tarry, wait for it; because it will surely come, it will not tarry.* (KJV) Hearing that and believing it, in 1997, I wrote that I would get my black belt in Kung Fu. In 1998 I wrote that I would start teaching. Both happened the same year I wrote them. I continue to write my vision every year.

In 1998 I started teaching Kung Fu to kids and Fitness Kickboxing to adults. I taught martial arts and continued working at the prison. In 2000 I retired from the prison, and my martial arts fitness center grew to be one of the largest and most recognized schools in South Florida. Since then, I have earned numerous black belts and instructor certifications. I have a 2nd-degree black belt in Judokickbox and am a Krav Maga, Haganah, Jeet Kune Do, and Muay Thai Kickboxing instructor. I also have a blue belt in Gracie Jiu Jitsu. I am a certified NRA and Israeli Tactical Shooting gun and rifle instructor. *I can do all this through him who gives me strength.* (Philippians 4:13 NIV)

My love for fitness continued. I've now been certified as a personal trainer, and the first kettlebell instructor training in Florida was done at my training center. I was the first person in South Florida to get certified in Indian clubs. I taught the first Fitness Kickboxing class in my area. I believe in being a student for life and have gotten many more fitness certifications. In 2014 I wrote a book, *Anta's Ageless Warrior Fitness,* and have been featured in numerous magazines and newspapers, and have appeared in over 100 television shows.

When you give it to God, He multiplies it and gives you back more.

After all these years, I continue to love bodybuilding, and since I had never taken a first-place, I felt that I still had unfinished business. So I started competing again in 2017 at 60 years old.

Satan did his best to stop me.

On June 19, 2016, I tore my chest in a bench press competition for repetitions in church.

Then, as I started preparing for the competition, two days after I began dieting, we heard that Hurricane Irma was coming toward Miami, so we decided to leave and go to Tennessee. As a result, I spent a week and a half eating healthy but was unable to stick to the diet while eating at restaurants.

Then, ten days before the South Florida Bodybuilding competition, as I was eating chicken, I took a bite and got this incredible pain in my right side molars. The dentist determined I had cracked a molar, and they had to extract the molar and give me antibiotics. Unfortunately, antibiotics retain water, which isn't good for competition. And I had to break my diet and go on bland food.

What else could go wrong?

On Thanksgiving, two days before the competition, I went to the emergency room with external, painful, bleeding hemorrhoids. I spent all day Friday in bed resting to be able to compete on Saturday.

Saturday came. I was weak and bleeding. But I competed and won. I won the South Florida Bodybuilding Championship 60+ Overall.

Then on December 4, I had surgery to remove the hemorrhoids. The devil can't stop what God has ordained.

Two years later, in 2019, another dream came true as I competed internationally. I was the runner-up in the North American Bodybuilding Championships 60+ Lightweight and the Florida State Bodybuilding Championships 60+. I believe that through the Christian lifestyle, eating healthy, and exercising, you can be as strong as in your youth—just like Caleb. Joshua 14:10-11 NIV, *Now then, just as the Lord promised, he has kept me alive for forty-five years since the time he said this to Moses, while Israel moved about in the wilderness. So here I am today, eighty-five years old! I am still as strong today as the day Moses sent me out; I'm just as vigorous to go out to battle now as I was then.*

My wife and I continue to actively serve God and His Kingdom. We have ministries in our church, Casa De Alabanza, Miami; I'm the head of the Safety Team Ministry; and I host a Band of Brothers Squad Men's group for my church. What Satan takes, God multiplies. Most of my accomplishments have come after I became a Christian. God has made my childhood dreams come true. And my self-image has gone from Charlie Brown to Superman. All praise and glory to God.

FAITH TO OVERCOME HURT

Many men have abandoned their relationship with God or their call to serve Him because they have been hurt and allowed the hurt to control their lives. And, in many instances, they have allowed the pain to crush their lives.

There is a large spectrum of hurts—emotional, physical, and circumstantial—which includes things like dealing with people or losing a friend or a relationship. Hurt can stem from changes in our lives, broken hearts, lost hope, aging, death, sickness, and other events that can encompass our minds.

It takes a radical step of faith to overcome hurt before it consumes you altogether. Many Christians have been conquered by hurt when they let their flesh get in the way. This one powerful word can quickly overcome us. So we must be on guard to war against fret, envy, anger, wrath, and evil. Hurt can cause us to fall prey to these actions and more. So, what is the solution to a man's hurting heart? Men are often so protective and guarded against allowing themselves to be vulnerable when dealing with past hurts. Do you think you could trust your hurting heart to someone who can help you?

God is your perfect solution—He never makes a mistake.

Someone who makes no mistakes and loves and cares about you IS always with you. Only God can handle every hurt supernaturally. God provides truth in His Word for you to hear. One of those truths is that God loves His children. His perfect love is all-encompassing. When one of His own is hurting, He knows it. When one of His sons is feeling pain, He feels it and He cares. God is a God of wisdom; He is also just and will always take action to protect His children.

> *If any of you lack wisdom, let him ask God, who gives generously to all without reproach, and it will be given him. (James 1:5 ESV)*

The first step in allowing God to handle your hurt is to trust Him and His wisdom, knowing He will guide you. The more you know Him, the more you will be open to trusting Him.

> *Keep trusting in the Lord and do what is right in his eyes. Fix your heart on the promises of God and you will be secure, feasting on his faithfulness. (Psalm 37:3 TPT)*

Men of Honor, please give your hurts and all that comes with them to God. All your past wounds will be covered with the healing power He so generously bestows on His children. If you are dealing with pain as a victim, recognize that the pain you experience from your past is not sinful. To blame victims for their pain is a sin against the wounded, the broken-hearted, and the oppressed. It is a sin against God Himself, whose heart is with those who are hurt. Our hurt hurts God, and He comes close to those who are broken-hearted. He confirms that in His Word in Psalm 34:18. Please hold the following scripture close if you are one who deals with tremendous hurt.

Even when bad things happen to the good and godly ones, the Lord will save them and not let them be defeated by what they face. (Psalm 34:19 TPT)

HENRY C. MERCY

Pastor Henry Claude Mercy, a native of Haiti, received his A.A. in Liberal Arts and Computer Science from College Bois-de-Boulogne, and his Bachelor of Theology from Acadia University & Bible Seminary College. He was ordained and earned a Master's in pastoral ministry in 2000 and is currently completing a Master's in Divinity at Freedom Bible College & Seminary.

His ministry began at Eglise Evangelique Baptiste Bethesda in Montreal, Canada, where he served for 12 years. He is a passionate communicator of the Word of God and speaks at numerous churches from Belle Glade to Miami, and has served at First Haitian Baptist Church of Sunrise, Providence of Grace, and Bethel Baptist Church. Henry Mercy's professional secular credentials include Case Manager, Resource Referral Specialist, and Family Advocate. He is now employed at the City of West Palm Beach.

Pastor Mercy is a servant with a heart of worship. He resides in the Palm Beach County area with his lovely wife, Joselie Marcellus, a Registered Nurse, and their four children—Danna, Shanika, Tevin, and Jose-Henry. They've been married for 28 years.

OVERCOMING ADVERSITY

BY HENRY C. MERCY

THE NEED TO BE

In a diversified and hectic world, any mistake can take you on the wrong path. Therefore, we must process quickly to best address social and personal challenges. As a young kid growing up, I needed a sibling to share my challenges or a father to answer my questions and doubts, but I had neither.

Growing up without a father was very challenging for me. The emptiness I constantly felt was overwhelming. Everything I experienced in life led me to believe that nothing could ever replace a father. During my childhood, I was so scared to ask questions, I did not feel comfortable being or becoming, and no one ever knew my doubts and shame. The more I wanted to become a normal kid, the more I wanted to have a father or a brother.

I grew up craving a way to express my need for love, to be somebody, and to have someone who would help guide me as I faced challenges. The Bible says, *Train up a child in the way he should go: and when he is old, he will not depart from it.* (Proverbs 22:6 KJV) How could a young kid like me shape his thoughts without guidance?

THE NEED TO BE TRAINED

I wish I had received the proper training to become the person I wanted to be. I wish I had a strong voice in my household to teach and play with me. But because I didn't, I had to learn how "to be" and eventually learn "to become." As a result, I have searched for love and validation. My single mother, with limited resources, gave me the best she could. She could not be my father figure, but she modeled how to prioritize God in my life. I was lonely most of the time, but I was encouraged to attend Sunday school weekly, and I encountered the Bread of Life, not in Bethlehem but in my home country, Haiti. I felt loved and accepted, even though I did not understand the magnitude of this encounter. But did I know what to do then? No. Becoming a young believer in Christ did not answer all my questions. I had more questions than answers. For example, I wanted to know why I was created, why I couldn't live in certain ways, what would happen to me in the next ten years, and how I would overcome something bad should it happen.

When I was a kid, fear was my constant companion and worst enemy. Fear was a silent but powerful force that prevented me from taking the next step. Even today, it is a struggle to take the next step, to change the status quo. I must always analyze and understand everything before making a decision. Throughout my days of questioning and fear, the only thing that has often kept me going is this verse: *God saved you by his grace when you believed. And you cannot take credit for this; it is a gift from God.* (Ephesians 2:8 NLT) Although I did not understand the concept of God's grace, I knew that believing in Him could change me and my situation. I looked up to church leaders, teachers, and other adults who appeared genuine to me. Deep inside, I wanted to be like them, speak like them, and become one of them.

THE NEED TO BE ANSWERED

I strongly believe that God placed people in my life to mold me the way He wanted me to be. Even though the clay had many questions for the Potter, some answers remained pending for years.

1. Who is God and where is He?

2. Why is He hiding from me?

3. Can He talk to me face to face?

4. Is He the Hero I have created in my heart, believing that life will be okay?

I had to learn to trust Him and pray every day, even when I had doubts. God answered some of my prayers. One day, I was in a fight at school. I was raised never to fight back but to walk away or report a problem to a teacher or an adult, so I was scared to go home after school because I knew my mom would punish me. The so-to-speak Hero who resided in my heart answered my prayers that day; I was not punished. God became a friend, and I realized that, by trusting in Him, I could control my fear and overcome it.

In my early years, I knew God could answer my prayers. My "need to be" grew deeper with a different thinking process. Should I call it "adversity"? I wondered how I would overcome it. I learned all I needed to do was to trust God. Proverbs 3:5-6, *Trust in the Lord with all your heart and lean not on your own understanding; in all your ways submit to him, and he will make your paths straight.* (NIV)

While trying to overcome fear and doubt in my infancy, I wondered where God was. While trying to be, I wondered what God was doing. He was a silent voice, sitting on the throne to guide me. The Psalmist said: *God is our refuge and strength, an ever-present help in trouble. Therefore we will not fear, though the earth give way and the mountains fall into the heart of the sea, though its waters roar and foam and the mountains quake with their surging.* (Psalm 46:1-3 NIV)

The ever-present assistance was always available to me, but my young faith could not grasp what God could do. God was a fortress to me when my life was forming and growing. He planted seeds in my heart and heard my cry for help.

With fear and doubts, my critical childhood years brought me to my teenage era.

THE NEED TO BECOME AND BELONG

In a stage of curiosity and growth, I had to overcome adversity. My teenage years were complicated; I carried fake treasures in my heart: fear, shame, cowardice, and loneliness. As an insecure teenager, I wanted to keep all I had; I did not want to trade treasures that caused me sorrow and pain. When you have nothing to be part of and nothing to lose, you keep what you have.

My mom had left to immigrate to New York. The quiet and shy teenager had to grow up quickly and make decisions. I had no drama and stayed out of trouble. Fear of disappointing my mother kept me going until I got a visa to Montreal, Canada. My adaptation to that beautiful and great land was tremendous. In a foreign country, my challenges were bigger than ever. I had to face a different environment, a different culture, and a different socio-political world. I had to learn how to fit in and go to school.

THE NEED TO BELONG

The people I lived with did not know the Lord, so it was not a priority to attend church or serve God as had been my custom. Instead, as a teenager in a beautiful environment, I wanted to explore and do things I had never done before. Without anyone to reprimand or guide me, my focus shifted. The new country offered me new opportunities to belong and fit in. My third-world country was history, and I felt the time had come to stand on something, even though I could not define what that something was. But I felt empty. My priorities had changed, and I convinced myself I didn't have to attend church to be a strong believer. I invented a new God to fit my needs. I had new friends in Montreal, and loneliness was not a problem anymore.

Yes, indeed, I belonged to my friends and their thoughts.

Life was different, and I aligned my plans with my friends and became one of them. It felt great, even though I had new doubts. What should I do, or why should I care? The answer is compelling: *Blessed is the one who does not walk in step with the wicked or stand in the way that sinners take or sit in the company of mockers, but whose delight is in the law of the Lord, and who meditates on his law day and night.* (Psalm 1:1-2 NIV)

What I learned:

1. The motive can be innocent, but bad company will corrupt you sooner or later.

2. Rooted in faith is not just a beautiful statement to voice but a practical stand in the storms of life.

3. You will never know how far you can go away from God unless you recognize your missteps.

4. A prayer life will keep you grounded in faith; it allows you to come before God without fear.

THE SECOND ENCOUNTER

It was snowing outside on a Saturday morning as I looked through the window, thinking how beautiful it was. While observing the scene's beauty, I played cards with an older friend in our household; he, too, had left God, so to speak. When he started singing hymns over and over again, I felt I had to speak out, and we had a warm conversation about the mighty God. I mentioned how I experienced God and used to attend Sunday school regularly and how God had answered some of my prayers. My friend stopped going to church for other reasons, but he told me he was ready to return to church.

We decided to find a church and start a new beginning with God. That afternoon, we walked through the snow slowly looking for a church. It was really cold, and I felt exhausted but relieved to find a place of worship. God had put us together to reignite the flame and come back to Him. The next day, we visited that church and later became active members.

I could not believe God placed me in a Haitian church ten minutes away from my new home, so far from Haiti. At that time, the church membership was around 350 people. It was a nice community of brothers and sisters devoted to serving Christ. Again, I had learned how to fit in, belong and find my way. The verses I had cherished in my heart a long time ago became alive again: *Trust in the Lord with all your heart and lean not on your own understanding; in all your ways submit to him, and he will make your paths straight.* (Proverbs 3:5-6 NIV)

1. I trusted God even though my faith had become somewhat lethargic.

2. My eyes were blinded by my new reality, and I was incapable of seeing what God was doing.

3. My heart was broken with a bitter taste I did not experience before.

4. My understanding was simply foolishness, but God had never forsaken me.

5. The invisible God had made my paths straight.

I had participated in several church activities, and one day after the sermon, the pastor called people to the altar. I decided to consecrate my life again to Christ.

I realized I needed to grow deeper with God and do away with the distractions that seized me. So I continued going to church and followed my pastor's leadership. I looked to him constantly; I watched how He lived with his family and treated them. I wanted that for me. He was the role model in my life, the brother I dreamed of, and a spiritual father to me.

God guided me to find a (spiritual) father from a distance but close to my heart, making the search for a physical father less important. The quiet kid became a teenager with a voice in a community of believers. While attending college (Bois-de-Boulogne College in Montreal, Canada), I became a youth leader, a Sunday school teacher, and a preacher. I was 18 years old the first time I delivered a sermon. I was so nervous I had a deep cramp, but I spoke for 30 minutes. After that sermon, people encouraged me, which was a shower of blessing.

My resilience started to evolve suddenly. I found my voice and tried to understand God's purpose. My past failures and doubts taught me how to face my demons.

Due to my immigration status, I soon had to return to my native land in humility. I swallowed my pride, expecting more from God. Again, when facing adversity, I asked God many questions. I should have been living in America. My mother had filed my immigration papers years earlier, but nothing had happened. Where was God?

We do not control adversity, the storms of life, or inconvenient surprises, but we can trust God to supply all our needs. This time, even though I had many questions, my patience toward God grew steadily. I knew God would intervene and speak to the storms on my behalf in due time.

What I learned in that stage is that storms can come at you from three different angles:

A) THE STORMS WE BRING ON OURSELVES

Impatience often drives us into crisis. When we get impatient, we often create a storm and run right into it. We fail to evaluate the cost and pay attention, and suddenly, we are in the middle of a storm.

B) THE STORMS GOD CAUSES

If God ordains a storm, it will occur no matter how much we pray. I strongly believe that sometimes the Mighty God orders a storm to teach us something or send us a message.

C) THE STORMS OTHER PEOPLE CAUSE

Sometimes people around us provoke the storm. You may do everything to stay out of trouble, but people in your life cause you to be in a violent storm.

I experienced all three types of storms. But God used each storm to help me grow deeper in faith. Fortunately, He did not fail me. Psalm 91:1 (NLT), *Those who live in the shelter of the Most-High will find rest in the shadow of the Almighty.*

OVERCOMING ADVERSITY THROUGH FAITH

My adversity came to an end, and I finally returned to my community of brothers and sisters in Montreal, Canada. I started school again, wanting to finish my education and earn a degree. This time, I decided to change my career. Instead of becoming a social worker, I chose to study Theology. I did not want to become a pastor, but it seemed God had always directed my path. I got married while in school and was blessed with four children. When unemployment hit home, I experienced a new level of storm in life; so I came to America to better myself, thinking I would eventually return to Canada.

It did not happen that way, however. I found a job to support my family financially, and years later, I found myself in ministry even though I was employed full-time. God knew how I felt about being a leader in a church. He knew how many times I had abandoned that calling, how many excuses I found not to lead a church. I was called by Grace Brethren to teach a small group of leaders to plant churches. I found excuses to quit and resigned from my position as an educator for church planting after three years. I had left the Haitian community to hide in an American church, but I never truly left. My world changed, and my adversities shifted, but God was always my heart's refuge. I needed to trust Him and live by faith through grace.

Being a father, husband, and church leader is not trouble-free; I realized that adversity is always looking for me in every corner of my life. When COVID-19 hit in early 2020, I got very sick and could not breathe properly. I was taken by ambulance to the hospital, not knowing how I would survive, but I did not give into fear. I remained calm and quiet. The physician did not explain to me how bad my condition was, but three days later, he came to my room and stated, "You are a miracle."

"What is that supposed to mean?" I replied.

He told me he had been convinced I would not make it. He had seen other patients in my condition, and they ended up going to the intensive care unit and dying. I was thankful to God because He spared my life even when I could not comprehend the danger I faced. Being a pastor carries a lot of stress in my community; the pastor answers all questions, gives direction, visits families, and calls the church members. Every decision made must be directed to the pastor for approval. The elders work hard also, but they consult the pastor for everything.

To prepare a weekly sermon and lead Bible study, the pastor must be ready, study and reflect, fight his own battle, and be on his knees praying for the congregates. Well, I am a husband too, a father who cares; should I pause and evaluate my life? How do I begin to balance my life with all the stress? Of course, I don't fear the troubles coming my way, but sometimes it is difficult to be, become, and belong. Now, my role model is far from me, and I do not look to fit in or have a voice. I became a pastor and a father, which both brought different struggles, but God never abandoned me. He always assisted me in overcoming my flaws. Yes, *with God all things are possible.* (Mathew 19:26 NKJV)

When I look back, my faith always played a role in my struggles. I have faced loneliness, fear, doubts, setback, and death. Did I have a strong faith to move the mountains? I cannot tell. But I am sure that God deserves all the credit. Anyone can trust Him like a child and make it to the finish line. Some will suffer, and others will face the waves of life and experience pitfalls or separation, but God can weather the storm with you. Here is what I have learned so far:

1. Faith keeps me grounded

2. Adversity keeps me rooted in faith

3. My Father in Heaven keeps things in perspective for me.

God's promise remains, Isaiah 41:10 (NIV), *So do not fear, for I am with you; do not be dismayed, for I am your God. I will strengthen you and help you; I will uphold you with my righteous right hand.*

DANIEL CUDONE

Daniel Cudone is an author, mentor, businessman, realtor, and newly married son of God who never thought he'd see his mountains moved. After 18 years following the Lord, his hunger for truth and righteousness taught him God is always faithful to finish what He starts. Daniel loves sharing the word of God and making waves in the business world. In his passion to bridge faith and financial stewardship to new levels, he truly believes possibilities are endless. He frequently speaks about the body of Christ supernaturally impacting all areas of personal life and society. Daniel sees the kingdom of God as reality and that earth should reflect the nature of God so Jesus can find faith everywhere. *Selah*

WHEN IDENTITY CALLS

BY DANIEL CUDONE

Not long ago, eighteen years ago, to be exact, I was a baby Christian. That seems like a long time, but in hindsight, it passed much quicker than my first eighteen years as a mere man. What does that mean, you might ask. Well, my perspective of who I truly am drastically changed when the Holy Spirit met me in a dark place. Even so, it's taken most of my Christ-minded existence to completely surrender to God's will for my life and realize I really was adopted into His household as His son. My point is that my IDENTITY in Christ was the most important revelation of my life, even though it's taken the second half of it even to begin capturing who God made me.

God's never-ending love towards me, while I have navigated through self-discovery, has been my saving grace. And along the way, He taught me there is no rush for what is good in His eyes. Without the blood

Jesus shed at the cross, we wouldn't have a chance at discovering God's individual plans for us, more or less appreciating the priceless journey. But in many cases, the best lessons and breakthroughs don't happen in overtly Christian or church-related arenas. God loves adventures. Allow me to explain.

As a single child in a traditional family, I did not grow up in a church-attending, spiritually-minded family. My father's side of the family is Italian, so naturally Catholic. My mother's side is Scottish and English, so they were Protestants. My mother and her siblings attended a Presbyterian youth group throughout their teens until college, but I never knew this until my twenties. God, Jesus, or even light church talk were not super important topics of conversation growing up. I had a slight clue about God due to attending "Christian" private schools and religious observations, like most people I knew. I even had Baptist friends who lived down the way from my house who would come and play video games and invite me to play baseball or football with other neighborhood kids. But I never fit in. It was very hard connecting to my peers, no matter the setting or age group.

From grade school through high school and even into my college years, I was constantly misunderstood and overlooked because I never put myself out there. Being rejected and sometimes bullied, I developed a complex and eventually pride as a protection mechanism. My response didn't do much except ensure that I would lie to myself and others about my inner feelings; the lies became ingrained as my reality after many years of hating myself and seeing life in darkness.

From about 8 to 15 years old, I started isolating myself and gravitated to complex hobbies where my quiet, geekier personality never felt challenged or even free to associate with outside influences. On top of that, just shy of my freshman year while attending a new high school, my parents were about to divorce. That opened me up to all sorts of insecurities and oppression, with raging hormones and high expectations to attain good grades. From 16 to 23, I gravitated to strange parties, promiscuity, light occult activities, pornography, horror films, and questionable company while doing recreational drugs and other things that were popular for my age group. In short, for as long as I could remember, I was severely depressed and alone inside. Many times, my mother would connect me with psychologists and psychiatrists in hopes of getting me to open up. Unfortunately, none of them really helped me change.

Being the only child in the house didn't make things easier, either. Being left alone and keeping secretive about my inner world turned out to be bad for me. One time a neighborhood boy attempted to form a sexual relationship with me. I found out many years later, to my surprise, that he had done the same with other people. Not loving myself allowed dark things into my world. I gave up on my education, hobbies, making friends, enjoying family, and I started giving up on life after not connecting personally or professionally anywhere. I truly had no clue as to my reality and certainly no clue about spiritual battles. When you feel lost, life feels chaotic, and when there is no aim or purpose, you stop moving forward.

Then, when I was 24, after losing the best corporate job I'd ever had and becoming fed up with my reality, Jesus came to me on a random August night in 2004. I had no knowledge of God's Kingdom, much less an understanding that Jesus wanted to save my life. But I soon realized God has zero limits on how He manifests Himself and little concern for man's opinion on how He brings salvation. He took me to church by making me His temple.

What do I mean by "church" or "temple" exactly? Is it the institution, the places we go Sunday morning? Is it the conferences, youth groups, prayer meetings, or whatever we label Christian? Not even close. YOU AND I ARE THE CHURCH BODY. We, the people, who are living stones, filled with the Holy Spirit and power, are the ecclesia saints God called and chosen for mighty exploits. We have treasure from on high within us that we can use to accomplish the impossible. We have the power, rite of passage, and duty to be salt and light everywhere, anytime God beckons. God moves in the grocery store, the campsite, race track, airport, stock market, public bathroom, and even in our sleep. The Word says, *The things which are impossible with men are possible with God.* (Luke 18:27 KJV) He needs us to see His macro vision for the world vs. a familiar micro church experience. God caters to the faithful and obedient who trust Him. The just shall live by faith and not by sight alone. We need constant clarity for God's bigger picture.

Earlier in my faith, when my spiritual growth and personal immaturity conflicted, I learned that no matter what you believe or practice, you're only as effective as your strongest reference point. Good or bad, people only act on what they know and understand. Many of God's people relegate the Holy Spirit to their logical reasonings and don't see His supernatural hand working. We often forget that the Bible is not just a book of God presenting stories and lessons but a book of principles and conduct that the Holy Spirit exclusively guides, as everything God does only abides in Spirit and truth. Yet as Christians, we are responsible for incorporating the Word of God exactly as it teaches. For example, we are to use His power in love and personal development, which in many cases can make us unpopular. But we are also to use our ability to dream, imagine better days and receive visions of wonderful things. Every good gift comes above, right? Not everything we gain in Christ comes with life-changing struggles, at least not the public kind. Often, God commissions opportunities to exercise faith while experiencing the pain of progress and avoiding the pain of regret. God knows our limited perspective, and He desires we all come to Him privately in daily relationship so He can do deep work in our hearts, thereby gaining everything in Him. God wants us to imagine still waters by green pastures and to walk in liberty and deliverance from our wounded past. But it costs us the limited knowledge we guard to possess His wisdom for grace.

GRACE...what is that? In totality, it's everything we receive by love, in place of what we deserve by condemnation. The scripture says, *There is therefore now no condemnation to them which are in Christ Jesus, who walk not after the flesh, but after the Spirit.* (Romans 8:1 KJV) Grace allows me to critique my life and my limitations, knowing prayer and fasting will bring me closer to Jesus so I can change for the better. Grace affords people time to mature, heal, believe, fail, start over, fail again, and rise above without religious fear that somehow God will give up on us. Concordantly, NO fruit of the Spirit gets its designation from "behavior modification." Please, at all costs, remember this! If that were the case, godly gifts like grace, mercy, favor, love, joy, peace, long-suffering, kindness, gentleness, goodness, meekness, temperance, and faith itself could be summarized as mental or emotional exercises. Nowhere in the Word of God does it say we make our own way through Christ, yet Christians sometimes suffer here. Behavior modification can spread like a virus when people, misunderstanding God's will, get sicker by self-assessed conclusions. Grace and mercy are part of God's love towards us so that we can stop acting like we're perfect and rest according to the finished work of the cross.

So, if we would slow down and really listen to God, we'd be shocked at how forgiving and caring He truly is, asking nothing but stillness to prove it. That's what resting is: leaning on God for His strength to capture you and mold your heart into a place where He can be received. Often, God is the kinder one compared to how we treat ourselves and others; He really is a good Father. He knows us more than we know ourselves. I can personally attest to that after years of hard-heartedness due to obstacles and situations beyond my control. Our identity in Christ is the key to knowing how to perceive and process life with God's eyes.

But sadly, many people see life not as it is but as they are internally— broken people in need of real healing, sometimes from serious trauma. It really can be a cocktail for disaster when pain and limited knowledge of God's love mix roots at the heart level. Our identities have often been the byproduct of family, friends, education, culture, entertainment, and whatever is common to man. But when we learn to rest in Him, we learn how to evaluate what's real over what's imagined. We learn that if God is given control of our lives, there are no failures or struggles that can truly harm us. We are no longer limited to the cares of this world. Jesus died so that we may have life and life more abundantly.

So why does it seem some people go further with God and succeed in their purpose-driven identity vs. some who try yet don't manage breakthrough?

The answer is SURRENDER. This is where the magic begins, and it is exclusively where everything falls into place. Even in my early Christian life, there was this yearning to grow deeper into the things of God. Little did I know that God had eyes on the heart of my issues. Later I began to realize His eyes were also on the heart of my victories. However, I had many obstacles from within that needed refining, or more accurately, needed to be put to death for the betterment of myself and others. God made me a resilient person with the intention of showing me tough but beneficial love where no one ever could. He did it in a way that resonated with lasting change by delineating that which was of Him, of me, and of Satan—essentially identifying that which influenced me vs. that which was my personal choice. As a man searching for God's embrace, this delineation helped me with self-forgiveness and compassion. However, most of my issues of attitude, worldview, ideals, desires, relationships, hobbies, self-worth, emotions, goals, eating habits, and even physical health still lingered. Imagine the load God took away when He showed me His forgiveness through Christ before I was even aware I needed forgiveness!

Our soul and body are separate yet inexorably connected aspects of our being, and they war against the Holy Spirit as often as allowed. From my late twenties until about the age of 35, God took me through a list of self-afflicted and spiritually-appointed wilderness experiences that really broke me for the better. I experienced everything from financial to relational difficulties and everything in between. God saw me through valleys to bring me to rivers of living water so only He could provide a remedy. Though it didn't seem that way or make sense till near my breakthrough, I never questioned Him. After years of personal, professional, ministerial, and relational victories, seeing myself as a truly capable and redeemed man of God became real. He even saw me fit to become a husband and successful businessman who makes generational wealth for his future children. Some Scripture that spoke to me throughout this time included 3 John 1:2, Deuteronomy 8:18, Matthew 6, Proverbs 4:20-27, Galatians 5, Philippians 4, and certainly Ephesians 6:10-20.

We have the opportunity to let go and let God make something beautiful in us, despite all the hurts of our past. He desires amazing things for us. However, the choice is yours to grant Jesus access into your heart to form you into the man He created you to be, whom you likely haven't met yet. Wild concept, huh?

When was the last time you did a personal reflection about your life? Are you intentionally stepping into your God-given identity? Sometimes, we don't fulfill an altogether perfect job of being "Men of Honor" in the long seasons, especially when everything seems delayed. Surrendering to God's fine-tuning in our lives and trusting His help will allow us to become perfect in His perfect time. God works even in our failures, and He never gets surprised when our little ideas fall short. This shows us that we can smile through the frustrations and remain humble for the next step. And along the way, we would do well to focus and not repeat old, dishonorable ways God rescues us from— because running around self-forming mountains is exhausting!

The Bible is raw and honest about human failings and, more importantly, about the forgiveness and sacrifice of a good Father that covers us in love. Every man, woman, and child is an imperfect but lovable creation. God's promises are designed to take us through refining fires so we can experience our greatest victories! The heat refines the beauty of our character. When we totally surrender to Christ, God will use all our circumstances for good. He knows our end from the beginning and sees us all as complete spiritual people made in His image. Jesus made room for everyone to explore life as an adventure so we can begin our 'new man' journey while trusting Him day to day!

God teaches that we must be Men of Honor who never quit—because He won't quit on us. He just needs a willing heart and a little faith to start the process!

FAITH TO OVERCOME PRIDE

God hates pride because it is a hindrance to seeking Him. Throughout scripture, the Bible talks about pride. Pride goes before the fall. *Too much pride will destroy you. You are better off to be humble and poor than to get rich from what you take by force.* (Proverbs 16:18-19 CEV) People are not to boast about themselves because when they do, they are no longer proclaiming the glory of God. What we say about ourselves means nothing in God's work.

In his pride the wicked man does not seek him; in all his thoughts there is no room for God. (Psalm 10:4 NIV)

It is what God says about us that makes the difference. Pride is giving ourselves credit for something that God has accomplished. Pride is taking the glory that belongs to God alone and keeping it for ourselves. Pride attempts to bring all the attention to us, consuming what is mastered in our lives with self-recognition.

> For who makes you different from anyone else? What do you have that you did not receive? And if you did not receive it, why boast as though you did not? (1 Corinthians 4:7 NIV)

We are taught as children to achieve, to accomplish, and to control our destiny by making a plan. We fight for the good grades, practice to get the big trophy, and fill our resumes, even in high school, to get into the best colleges. And then we revel in our achievements.

But there is a difference between confidence and pride, and that difference comes from our very roots.

God warns us about pride (*Pride and arrogance and the way of evil and perverted speech I hate.* – Proverbs 8:13 ESV). Pride is an arrogant conceit, a tunnel vision that proclaims that I alone can accomplish any feat I put my mind to. It is a deep satisfaction that comes from the well of self-absorption and is born of anxiety and the need for accomplishment and perfection.

Confidence, on the other hand, is believing that I am who God says I am; therefore, I am sure of my success. (*Though a mighty army surrounds me, my heart will not be afraid. Even if I am attacked, I will remain confident.* - Psalm 27:3 NLT) The sustenance for confidence is God himself—our sustainer, strength, and guide. And it comes with the caveat that in order to be truly successful, we must surrender to God's will and follow His direction.

How can we walk away from the pride of self and walk into the confidence of being a man of God? Our biggest weapon is honesty and truth. When we examine our own lives honestly in front of God, we will begin to see that we never, ever have done anything completely by ourselves! If you got great grades, you likely have a teacher, parent, or even taxpayers to thank for providing you with a great education! If you won that championship, chances are there was a coach guiding you and teammates cheering you on! If your high school resume afforded you a scholarship to the finest school, likely there was a counselor, student, pastor, or friend supporting you along the way!

An honest reflection will take each of these instances a bit further and reveal that it is God himself who blesses us with people, intelligence, talent, skill, and resources!

The fact is that without God, even the best of our intentions would be useless. Turning our backs on our pride allows us to turn and see the glory of the One who deserves all the credit: our God! Our infinite, unchanging, all-powerful, all-knowing, perfect in power and wisdom, faithful, merciful, gracious, loving, and glorious Father. He is our source and our strength. In that, we can stand proud! We can hold honor in our hearts as men, knowing we relinquish all boastful acts of fleshly acknowledgement to the One who deserves all the credit. God has allowed us each to be "that person" He has created. What good has He not helped you achieve? Give Him the praise.

> For we are God's masterpiece. He has created us anew in Christ Jesus, so we can do the good things he planned for us long ago. (Ephesians 2:10 NLT)

TRENT CAMPBELL

 Trent Campbell is a follower of Jesus Christ. Born in North Alabama to two amazingly wonderful parents, Trent grew up in Southeast Louisiana on a family farm. He met his beautiful gift from the Lord, Mindi, and they married in January 1993. Together they have two children, Karley and Cody, and are now celebrating their first grandchild.

Trent grew up in the church. Working hard and fearing God was the constant compass of his family. In the late 90s, his life began to become empty and void. He had a "knowledge of Christ" but had not made a decision to follow Him unapologetically. He had the knowledge but not the Power of Christ. In 1997, Trent completely surrendered to God's Kingship and has never been the same since. He quit farming in 2015, and the church he was pastoring became his home. Trent and his family moved to south Alabama where they currently reside. He is so grateful to have the opportunity to be an encouragement to you.

BATTLING FORWARD IN FAITH

BY TRENT CAMPBELL

Once, I heard a pastor say that, in a way, we are all like Joseph in Genesis chapter 40. We are headed into a Pit experience, in the middle of a Pit experience, or coming out of a Pit experience. I relate to that, and I'm sure you probably can, too.

If you have decided to follow Jesus, I'm sure Satan, our adversary, has added some difficulties to your walk of faith. But overcoming adversity through faith is a whole lot easier said than done. James chapter 1:2-4 (TPT) tells us that when our faith is tested, we should be joyful, excited, and even call it a gift. But how do we do that?

When we follow God and His Word, we often assume, in our failed human logic, that because we've received Jesus Christ as our Savior, we will no longer have any problems, and somehow, we will be immune to trouble. However, we soon discover that this is not true. Troubles do come, and problems do happen. Adversity comes to all of us. But perhaps how we respond to our troubles determines how long they stay and how they affect us.

Joseph himself—you know, Joseph from the Pit in Genesis 40?—is a fitting example of the above concept. Joseph went through all kinds of horrible situations, like betrayal by family members, sexual assault accusations, and abandonment of a friend even while he was in the pit. And yet, throughout it all, Joseph trusted God. And Scripture tells us over and over that the Lord was with him. Because of his steadfastness to God, God exalted Joseph to a position of authority and used him to save the nation of Israel from a severe famine.

Four hundred years later, the children of Israel also exemplified the importance of our response in times of trouble. God used an ex-murderer named Moses to deliver the Israelites from generations of slavery, but their attitude was less than grateful and faithful. Exodus 13 tells us that God used Moses to lead the children of Israel in a roundabout way so that they would not get discouraged from adversity. But despite God's provision, as the journey continued and they reached the land God had promised them, they refused to enter, bending to fear rather than relying on faith. As a result, God continued to teach them as they wandered in the wilderness for 40 years.

We can often feel like God is leading us into more problems than we had before we headed toward our promised land, right? May I share with you something I have learned to live by? "Feelings are real, but they are not necessarily the truth." In other words, just because we do not see God's help or direction through our natural senses does not mean He is not moving us in the right direction. Hebrews 11:1

UNITED MEN OF HONOR:
OVERCOMING ADVERSITY THROUGH FAITH

(AMP) says faith doesn't come from our physical senses; faith comes from the spirit of God. This kind of faith and trust comes only from a relationship with our heavenly Father through his Son Jesus by the Holy Spirit.

Looking back over my life, I can see many times when I felt like God was not at all working in my life. But of course, now I recognize that this is absolutely not true. My wife and I got married in 1993 and farmed for about 25 years in southeast Louisiana. God blessed us with two wonderful children. We worked hard and spent most of our lives on those dusty gravel roads of southeast Louisiana. I also pastored a small local church and gave it my all. Life was simple but very demanding. It seemed as though my life would always be about farming and following God. Then, in 2010, it all seemed to be coming to an end as God was closing the door on our farm life. So, you can understand that I began to feel that God somehow was making a huge mistake. I had feelings of, *Lord, you must not understand what is going on.* How silly I must have seemed to Him at times.

In the spring of 2011, we sold all of our cows. We had been feeding 973 cows about 50,000 pounds of feed a day, and, just like that, it was over. I remember, like yesterday, that feeling of *Thank you, Jesus, and Oh my goodness, what is about to happen?* All at the same time, I felt *What now? Where now? What if?* Fear began to flood my life. It felt like we were leaving Egypt but headed in the wrong direction. We had prayed and believed for God to lead us, and I wanted so badly to be in God's will for our family life. Proverbs 3:5-7 says to trust in the Lord completely. I did, right up to the moment that I had to leave. Then I wanted to rely on my *own* understanding, opinions, and feelings. Let me tell you that it's been 11 years since the last load of cows pulled out. And the celebration of my deliverance from 25 years of a 24/7 dairy farm workload quickly turned into months of doubting fear. I would be lying if I said that I didn't act exactly like the children of Israel at times.

God sees the end from the beginning. We only see in part all that He has in store. Without faith, it is impossible to please God, Hebrews 11:6 tells us. I see I had faith, but I was looking at the circumstances much like Peter did when Jesus asked him to come out on the water. When Peter looked down and took His eyes off Jesus, he began to sink. I was looking at circumstances and allowing fear to control my feelings. 2 Timothy 1:7 tells us that God has not given us a spirit of fear but of power, love, and a sound mind! I rebuked the spirit of fear within me and commanded him to leave my mind, my family, and every other area of my life. I made a conscious decision to trust God and His Word for my life.

There is no overcoming adversity unless we use faith, the faith that God has given us. Change in this life is necessary. It must come, and it will. United Men of Honor has committed to helping men all over the world overcome this adversity through faith in God by being a source of hope, encouragement, and support as God leads you and me into His promises. Jeremiah 29:11 says that God knows the plans He has for each of us, plans of hope for a future. I encourage you not to give up your destiny—your future. It's just on the other side of your adversary, but it will take faith to reach it—faith in HIS WORD. TRUST in HIS PROVISION, persevere through trials, and endure to the end. God's Word tells us in Revelation chapters 2 & 3 that those who endure and persevere, the followers of Jesus who are relentless in our pursuit, will receive ALL He has promised.

Maybe you have not ever committed to following Christ. Perhaps you feel hopeless, helpless, and too far gone to be a Christ-follower. But, I'm telling you right now, wherever you are, God is waiting with open arms to receive you. His Word promises if we will turn to Him and sincerely ask Him to be the Lord of our lives, He will come into our lives according to Revelation 3:20 and Romans 10:8-11.

Will you pray this prayer with me IN FAITH right now? Just simply say out loud, "Lord, I humbly come before you. I realize I have turned my back on you and your Word. I ask, Heavenly Father, for your forgiveness of all my sin against you. I believe in my heart and confess with my mouth that you sent your Son Jesus to die on a cross for my sin. I believe He was placed in a tomb, and three days later, He rose from the grave and now sits at your right hand. Jesus, I choose you today as my Lord, and I ask you, Holy Spirit, to guide and lead me every day as I courageously follow you. In Jesus' name, AMEN!!!"

Congratulations and welcome to the family of God. You just made the most crucial decision in your life!

Now, getting God's Word into your life is vital to building upon the decision you have made. We are praying for you and want to help you continue in your new journey with our Lord and Savior Jesus Christ! Contact us here at United Men of Honor to share your story and battle forward with us.

DR. MICHAEL WOLFORD

Dr. Michael Wolford is board certified in internal and emergency medicine and an ordained minister of the Gospel for the Assemblies Of God Church. He graduated from Philadelphia College of Osteopathic Medicine, did his residency at the University of Medicine and Dentistry in New Jersey, and has worked as a full-time emergency room physician for the past 30 years.

Dr. Wolford also holds a bible degree from Global University and has gone on numerous medical mission trips to the Amazonia Regions of South America, the Southern Continent of Africa, and the South Pacific. Due to his efforts, he was honored as the International Humanitarian of the Year by the Palm Beach County Medical Society. He also regularly works with Prayer Stations around South Florida and loves to speak about how his Lord has impacted his life.

Dr. Wolford currently lives in Jupiter, Florida, and works at West Palm Beach VA Medical Center. He can be reached at mwolford98@aol.com and is looking forward to hearing from his readers. He would love to hear how his story has impacted your life.

YET!

BY DR. MICHAEL WOLFORD

Ever since I was a little child—from the age of five—I wanted to be a physician.

When the time came, I applied to two colleges. I was placed on the waiting list at Gettysburg, but I got accepted to Susquehanna University. So I chose SU and became involved in the Christian world there. In September 1986, my senior year at the university, I was involved in the new presidential induction ceremony. The induction ceremony had many representatives from colleges and universities across the United States. One of those representatives was CF, who happened to be the admissions director of Philadelphia College of Osteopathic Medicine. So, I took the opportunity to introduce myself to her.

Fortunately, within just a few weeks, I was granted an interview, and by October 1986, I was accepted into medical school. I eventually chose to do my internship at Millcreek Community Hospital in Pennsylvania, which was a difficult time both mentally and physically. During this time, I got involved in a local church, and, at a church event, I met the woman who would become my future wife. After a whirlwind romance that lasted only a few months, I asked her to marry me, and we planned our wedding for October 1991.

In the beginning, we had a usual marriage. We had three children and, leaning into my career, I opened my first practice in medicine. Honestly, though, my wife and I never really took the chance to get to know each other. I was not a very good communicator. I assumed a lot of things and expected a lot of things. I knew I was not happy in the marriage, and though we went to counseling, we never really became very close.

While our children were still young, we moved from Western Pennsylvania to Florida. As a family, this is where our troubles really began. My wife never wanted to move to Florida; she did not like being far from her family and missed them greatly. So, on every possible occasion over the next ten years—spring break, Christmas break, and summer—she took the kids to Pennsylvania while I stayed behind and worked. I was always disappointed. I worked so many hours, providing for our growing family budget, and I became more and more angry at the situation. This anger reared its ugly face on a regular basis. I lost my temper a lot, yelled regularly, and most of the time, I was not a pleasant individual to be around. As a result, our marriage continued to fall apart.

Despite looking like a very successful professional, I was tremendously depressed. I felt like nothing I did was enough and that I was inadequate as a husband, a father, and a person. My wife and I lived separate lives in the same house. We had not shared a bedroom for four years. And eventually, I had an adulterous affair with a massage therapist I barely knew. Although I tried to cover it up, it exposed itself. At that point, my wife and I started living truly separate lives in the most uncomfortable, untrustworthy, frustrating, and depressing circumstance I could have ever imagined. That is when I became suicidal.

One night, I went to a private place with my loaded 40 caliber handgun, ready to end everything. I sat with the gun on my lap for well over half an hour. A couple of times, I pointed it at my head and then laid it back down. I felt completely alone as I sat in the absolute darkness—distant from everyone in the universe. I was embarrassed and humiliated by the circumstances that got me there. I regretted the adulteress relationship tremendously, but I was even more regretful that my wife now knew. As I was sitting there, I just wanted to end it all! I wanted to escape my circumstances, my marriage, and my family.

But then, shockingly, a glimmer of light shined through an open door. Suddenly a Christian song I had previously listened to on occasion started running through my mind. That song helped carry me through that very ugly and dark night, and it would also help me through much of the horrific tragedy that lay ahead. As *Wasteland* by NEEDTOBREATHE filled my mind, I started crying my eyes out, and I gently removed the weapon from my lap. And I said to my Lord, "I feel distant now, I feel alone now, I feel so horribly remorseful and so full of regret, but You and I can do this! We can get through this ugly time."

Over the next few months, things didn't get any easier at the house. Divorce was imminent! A couple of times, the police were called to the house. I reached out to my parents, who lived in Pennsylvania, and explained the circumstances. My father stepped in—he came to Florida and moved into the house, hoping to help keep the peace. I planned to move in with a friend, and he started helping me pack up boxes.

Eventually, my wife told me she was filing for divorce. She showed me around our house and made a list of all our handmade Amish furniture, informing me she was planning on taking every single piece. I very peacefully walked around listening to everything she had to say, although I was fuming inside. Afterward, I went to bed, but I could not sleep. After everyone was asleep, I left the house, not knowing I wouldn't return for over five months.

Trying to decompress one February evening, I started driving around the neighborhood, and then I headed to the highway. I stopped at a bar, had a few drinks, and then decided to return home, but I never made it. I hit the roundabout and multiple curbs as I entered our development, going over 75 miles per hour.

After the accident, I couldn't feel or move my legs. I just leaned against the outside of the driver's door until help arrived. The police notified my father of the accident and immediately transferred me to the local trauma center. My father arrived at the emergency room shortly thereafter—no one else from my family ever came.

I had fractured seven vertebrae, including a burst fracture of T12, which caused a spinal cord injury, making me a paraplegic. I had multiple very unstable spinal fractures and had surgery the following morning. Everything in surgery went very well, but though I had no injury to my lungs or chest, the doctors could not take me off the ventilator—a condition that was very confusing to the entire medical staff. I remained on the ventilator for another seven weeks, developing Guillain-Barre syndrome, which caused my diaphragm, the muscle responsible for breathing, to become paralyzed. More than once during that period, I took many turns for the worse. My parents were convinced that if my wife had the opportunity to shut off the ventilator, she would have.

I never got off the ventilator at the trauma center but was transferred four weeks later to a chronic ventilator rehab facility. It took that facility another three weeks to get me off the ventilator. Then, a few days later, I was transferred to a spinal cord injury rehab facility. That facility was Brooks Rehabilitation in Jacksonville, Florida, about 300 miles from everyone I knew.

My dad followed me to Brooks. I was given a small suite with another bed in the room. I was in a turtle shell brace – a thoracolumbar brace that needed to be secured before I could get out of bed. I could not urinate on my own, and I could barely feed myself. My hands were contractured from being immobile for so long, and I had so much pain—excruciating pain every night. Sometimes I felt like my hands and feet were on fire. But my father was there day and night at my side. He would rub my hands and feet with lidocaine cream, many nights even falling asleep beside me in his chair. The days were long at Brooks. I had leg, speech, swallowing, and cognition retraining sessions. I had lost 50 pounds.

Over the next month, there were times I was very down, but always my father was there. I developed a relationship with him that we never had before. At the same time, I developed a relationship with my Father in heaven like I never had before. I was absolutely dependent on Him. I was almost forced, but I willingly surrendered everything and every part of my life to Him—my finances, my home, my car, my career, my family, my children—absolute everything.

After four weeks, my biological father left to travel back home. At first, I was so angry with him.

I made one of my first online posts, which said:

> "I rejoice today, not because it's Sunday, but because of so many things happened. First of all I slept the entire night last night. When breakfast arrived, I actually opened up a can. Now my hands have been so weak I have not been able to make a fist ever since my injury. I would have to use the backside of a spoon or a fork or knife or something to get the tab of the can open. Then I had my physical therapy this morning at 9 AM. I have no video of this since no one was around to take one but I actually walked 1000 feet this morning. I walked around all four of the stations - 200 feet. I was able to walk around the entire lap of nursing stations three times which is 600 feet, then I took a brief rest, walked another two laps which is another 400 feet. Now many of you reading this may take this for granted, I don't any longer. The therapist asked me what I wanted to do it today. I said WALK! I also call that a reason to rejoice. I went from being very discouraged to have many things to rejoice God is good, He has

taken care of me in the past, He saved my life. God is preparing me for one of the greatest testimonies [a] person can ever have, I can't wait for that time to come. God still has a lot of work to finish. God promised He will be faithful to complete the work He began."

I remember writing that like it was just a few weeks ago. Don't get me wrong, life was still very tremendously hard. I tried getting out of bed on my own once; I had just started walking and thought I could finally do it on my own, but I fell. I crawled on the floor over to the nightstand; it took every bit of strength in me to get off the floor. Then I shuffled over from the nightstand to the bed. I was sweating profusely.

A nurse arrived in the room. She asked, "What's wrong, Michael?"

I politely said, "Nothing, just nothing."

She doubted my response, just nodded her head, and left the room.

After several weeks, it was time to be transferred to my final rehab facility. But my insurance terminated the high-level care I had been receiving and insisted I be transferred to a lower-skilled facility. So, I was sent to Chatsworth Skilled Nursing Facility. Finally, I was back near my home and was able to get visitors. My cousin came and brought me a book, *The Strength You Need,* by Robert Morgan. Another friend had brought me another book, *The Comeback,* by Louie Giglio.

There, in every way imaginable, God made Himself known to me as a miracle-working, promise-keeping provider. Listen to me here. Everything I am going to tell you happened! It was real! I got off the ventilator on March 27, 2017. For the next two days, I hallucinated.

After I started seeing and thinking normally, I found out I was a paraplegic; and then I had a vision. Every time I closed my eyes, I saw this statement written on a chalkboard:

"If you lose your wife, your family, your home, your car, your job, your pension—everything—I am enough. No! I AM MORE THAN ENOUGH!"

I must have seen this vision more than 1000 times over four months. After that, the vision slowly faded away. As I struggled to move my hands and get in and out of bed with feet that didn't move and with a tracheostomy and breathing struggles, I knew one thing for certain! God alone was more than enough!

I wasn't sure if I would ever return to being an emergency room physician, but I wanted to make a comeback to something!

God kept speaking to me in many ways, including through the books I had been given. I was now on chapter 9 of *The Comeback*, titled "Jesus is Enough." WOW! Jesus is Enough! I had already been seeing this repeatedly in visions. Now it was in the book. Jesus alone is enough. The book kept crescendoing, and I wanted to know what ending God had in store for me.

God also used the book *The Strength You Need*. Each chapter brings out a somewhat remote Bible verse and talks about it. One chapter that stuck out and hit me hard was a chapter talking about Habakkuk, chapter 3:17-19 (NIV):

> *Though the fig tree does not bud*
> *and there are no grapes on the vines,*
> *though the olive crop fails*

and the fields produce no food,
though there are no sheep in the pen
and no cattle in the stalls,
yet I will rejoice in the Lord,
I will be joyful in God my Savior.
The Sovereign Lord is my strength;
he makes my feet like the feet of a deer,
he enables me to tread on the heights.

In these verses, a man lost everything. But he does not complain, doesn't get angry, doesn't speak with regret, and doesn't get frustrated. Instead, he says, "YET" I will rejoice! Those three letters – YET, are three letters of a very small word that has encouraged me to this day. YET!

While I was in a wheelchair, while I could barely move, while I wasn't sure if I was going to lose everything, I knew one thing for absolute certain. My Lord was a mighty God, a God who was a more-than-enough-God. A God I would choose to serve YET losing almost everything.

God miraculously allowed my body to start walking again. By September 2017, I was able to return to work part-time. And by March 2018, I was YET again a full-time emergency room physician.

Life doesn't always take the turns we want it to. Yes, I did get divorced. Yes, for a season, I did lose contact with my children. Yes, I did lose my house. Yes, I did lose my car. YET through it all, God was by my side. My Lord showed me favor, grace, and mercy in so many phenomenal ways. He transformed me from an angry man full of bitterness, rage, hostility, and resentment to the individual I am today—a gentle, caring, kind, emotionally stable, and appreciative person.

No matter what you might be going through, I want to remind you we have a miracle-working God who cares tremendously. He loves you and will provide everything you will ever need. Our God, knowing I needed something extra, something supernatural, provided in a way that only He could. Through the vision He gave me day in and day out, I knew that no matter what loss would come my way, He was more than enough. YES, we have a more-than-enough-God. I now daily praise my Lord for who He is—He a Great and Mighty God who alone deserves our praise. He brought joy in my step – when steps were hard to come by.

My Lord supernaturally healed me. He healed this body physically and emotionally to do whatever work He called me to do. My goal is to never let my Lord, my Healer, my Redeemer, my Savior, and my Best Friend down.

I hope that by sharing some of my greatest struggles, weakness, and failures with you, you might also realize our Lord is not done with you YET! Those three letters – YET.

My Lord has restored much of what I lost, but stuff doesn't matter. Stuff is folly in the Lord's eyes. What our Lord had in store for me was an absolute surrender – absolute. That means if I lost everything, yes everything, and had absolutely nothing earthly but my Lord, that would be enough. No, that would be more than enough!

AFTERWORD

As you step out to overcome adversities through faith every day you live, keep standing your ground, decreeing your victory no matter what you see right now. There will be sudden displays of triumph in your life as you follow Him in honor and respect. You can count on it—because as you have read this book, the authors have prayed for you. They prayed that God would open cages of limitations that imprison you and infuse you with His power, enabling you to overcome strong temptations. They have prayed that any addictions, identity issues, fear, intimidation, depression, or anxiety that lurks would be released and that sin, which so easily attacks, would suddenly be contained. You have been fully equipped with the "whole armor" to battle, conquer, and live a victorious, overcoming life to influence the world for generations.

What do you have to look forward to as God's warrior? For one, your enemy (Satan) will be reminded through you over and over that victory is in the resurrection of the Son of God (Jesus). Also, Satan will recognize the Holy Spirit's power in you, giving you the rights of sonship and the assurance to fight the battle and WIN.

We hope you have encountered God's heart for mankind as you have read these stories of men claiming victory from secret places that God has led them through. May your hidden strengths be awakened to see the awesome power of God, and may you trust Him if He calls you to share your battle and struggle to help another brother or friend. Remember the scripture Revelation 12:11, *And they overcame him (the enemy) by the blood of the Lamb, and by the word of their testimony.* (KJV)

Despite what has happened in your past or what you currently encounter, God promises a future full of hope and blessings. But that future will not happen on its own. You are responsible for some things, such as prayer, putting on the armor, trusting not leaning, and obeying His guidelines. God will help you with these if you only ask Him.

God has a plan for your future, but so does your enemy—whose intentions are not good! The devil's plan can not succeed if you're walking and talking with God, living in obedience, honoring Him, and standing firm in His Word (that's your sword)! Despite what is happening around you, your enemy, the devil, will be defeated, but he will try to wreak havoc until he is. Ask God for strength and endurance to continue in what you must do. Don't give up or give in. Remember, if you start getting consumed by present battles in your life and feel like you are going nowhere, God has your back! God is preparing you for what is next. Don't lose heart.

The Lord is near to all who call upon Him, to all who call upon Him in truth. He will fulfill the desire of those who fear (respect) Him; he hears their cry and saves them. (Psalm 145:18-19 NIV)

God wants to equip you to do a new mission, and as the doors of opportunity begin to swing open, keep doing what is right. When you least expect it, God will show you your assignment.

Remember, you can do all things through Christ who strengthens you, but you must take the first step through faith to overcome adversity and move you from where you are. You can do this! Step out in faith, remembering... *With God all things are possible.* (Matthew 19:26 NKJV)

If God has moved within you through reading this book, prompting you through the power of the Holy Spirit to be brave and share your story, we want to hear from you. We can help you get your story to the world. Contact us at www.unitedmenofhonor.com or @ UnitedMenofHonor on social media.

May God do exceedingly, abundantly, beyond what we can ever imagine according to His power at work within us.

No man shall be able to stand before against you all the days of your life. Just as I was with Moses, so I will be with you. I will not leave you or forsake you... Be strong and very courageous, being careful to do according to the law that Moses my servant commanded you. Do not turn from it to the right hand or to the left, that you may have good success wherever you go... For then you will make your way prosperous, and then you will have good success. Have I not commanded you? Be strong and courageous. Do not be frightened, and do not be dismayed, for the Lord your God is with you wherever you go. (Joshua 1:5,7-9 ESV)

Be brave. You've got what it takes!!!

UNITED MEN OF HONOR. TOGETHER WE CAN.

MORE FROM WPP!

World Publishing and Productions was birthed in obedience to a calling by God. Our mission is to empower the writer and artist to walk in their God-given purpose as they share their God story with the world. We offer one-on-one coaching and a complete publishing experience. God has gifted us each with unique gifts and stories that were meant to be shared.

To find out more about how we can help you become a published author or to purchase books written to share God's glory, please visit:

www.worldpublishingandproductions.com